# THE OXFORD MOVEMENT IN SCOTLAND

# THE OXFORD MOVEMENT IN SCOTLAND

by

W. PERRY, D.D.

*Dean of Edinburgh*

With a Foreword by

THE MOST REVEREND
THE PRIMUS OF THE EPISCOPAL CHURCH
IN SCOTLAND

✠

CAMBRIDGE
AT THE UNIVERSITY PRESS
1933

**CAMBRIDGE**
**UNIVERSITY PRESS**

University Printing House, Cambridge CB2 8BS, United Kingdom

Cambridge University Press is part of the University of Cambridge.

It furthers the University's mission by disseminating knowledge in the pursuit of education, learning and research at the highest international levels of excellence.

www.cambridge.org
Information on this title: www.cambridge.org/9781107437883



First published 1933
First paperback edition 2014

*A catalogue record for this publication is available from the British Library*

ISBN 978-1-107-43788-3 Paperback

*To*

THE RIGHT REVEREND

HARRY SEYMOUR REID, D.D.

BISHOP OF EDINBURGH

in thankful recognition of a long and
happy friendship
and in admiration of a Father in God
as ready in sympathy as he is
steadfast in hope

# PREFACE

To give full and balanced reasons for all the statements and to quote references for all the facts contained in this book would require a prohibitively expensive volume. I have done my best to be accurate as to the facts and at least frank in my judgment of many questions on which more views than one are possible. The reader will do well to study Dean Church's classic entitled *The Oxford Movement*, which, however, is limited to a description of the critical events of the first twelve years in Oxford. The approaching Centenary Celebration has called forth a number of books which carry the history of the Movement in England down to the present day; of these one of the best is by Canon Sparrow Simpson.

I am much indebted for valuable assistance to the Rev. C. L. Broun, M.A., the Rev. W. D. Cooper, B.D., Miss Anne Ashley, M.A., and Miss Isabel C. Grieve.

W. Perry

*All Saints' Day*, 1932

# CONTENTS

CONTENTS

## CHAPTER IV

## BEGINNINGS AND THE FIRST PUBLIC SCHOOL IN SCOTLAND

1833–1857



## CHAPTER V

## TWO YOUNG CATHEDRAL BUILDERS



## CHAPTER VI

## A SCOTTISH PUSEY

# FOREWORD

## BY THE MOST REVEREND THE PRIMUS

I venture to commend this book to the careful study of our Church people. Much has been written about the Oxford Movement of 1833 in histories and biographies. But these mainly had in view the influence of the Movement in relation to the Church of England. We are greatly indebted to the Dean of Edinburgh for sketching for us its influence upon the thought and life of our Church in Scotland.

It is important to note:

(1) That in its origin the aim of the Movement was to elicit a revival of loyal obedience to the principles and system of the Church as contained in the Prayer Book and its formularies. It cannot be too often insisted that the primary purpose of the Oxford leaders was a spiritual revival, evidenced in a disciplined life of personal devotion, prayer, worship and for the clergy of study and faithful pastoral work.

(2) How soon knowledge of the Movement reached the Church in Scotland in spite of the difficulties of communication a century ago. A copy of the statement on doctrine drawn up at the

meeting held at Hadleigh in July 1833 was sent to the Scottish Bishops and drew forth their cordial approval. They said it was what they had always taught.

(3) That not a few of the younger English clergy of that time were depressed and unsettled by the Erastianism and worldliness of the Church of England and were attracted to the Church in Scotland by reason of its greater freedom.

(4) A still more interesting point is the prominence of many of the Scottish laity, not only in accepting the aims and putting into practice the principles of the Movement themselves, but also in striving to promote and spread them throughout the Church. To explain these aims and elucidate these principles is one of the chief purposes of Dr Perry's work.

With such points in our minds as we read this book, I suggest that it should provoke many questionings both for those of us in the ministry and for our laity. The years that followed the beginning of the Movement in the Scottish Church were a time of real renewal, activity and generosity in our Church life. If the study of this book can do something to call forth a similar renewal in our day, it will amply have fulfilled its purpose.

CHAPTER I

# The Method of Revival

In the long history of the Church the revival of religion has taken many different forms, but never so simple a form as that adopted by the Oxford leaders in 1833. They had the audacity to ask bishops, priests and laypeople to be consistent with the teaching of their own Church. It seemed a very poor method compared with other great revivals that had gone before. It was quite unlike that of John Wesley with its open-air preachings, its boisterous demonstrations, and thrills of conversion. To tell people simply to believe what they profess and to practise what they believe appears to be the most trite of counsels. Yet when all is said, that is the root of the matter in a Christian country in which habit and custom may have made religion dull and flat. All religious revivals, if they do not begin there, reach that simple plea for consistency sooner or later.

In England the relation between Church and nation was a curiously intimate one at the beginning of the nineteenth century. The belief was that an Englishman *quâ* Englishman was a member of the Church of England. The national Church existed to do certain things for him, mainly to baptise, marry and bury, and conduct services for his edification when he felt inclined to attend them. The Church of England was in fact an ethical adjunct of the nation; its chief officers, the bishops, were appointed by the Crown, the stipends of the clergy bore a sinister resemblance to taxes since, like them, they were collected under processes of strict law, its ministrations of Baptism, Marriage and Burial were recorded in State forms, its Book of Common Prayer was the book annexed to an Act of Parliament. Nation and Church, Englishman and Churchman, birth and Baptism were names for the same things.

Out of this strange mixture of the national and religious, Keble, Newman and Pusey evoked a revival of religion so remarkable, that in thirty years it not only awoke the Church to a sense of its Divine mission and compelled the nation to recognise it, but also moved to a new life of passionate devotion and social service multitudes of people who before had treated God as a pious hypothesis and their neighbours as those with whom they had nothing to do.

How did these men achieve this miracle? To begin with; they took the situation as it was. In effect they said,

"The people of England belong to the Church of England, they acknowledge the vogue if not the authority of the Book of Common Prayer. Well then, what has this Book to say about the Church? Does it regard the Church as a department of the State which the government of the day can use according to its convenience? Does this Book say that a bishop's chief function is to sit and talk in the House of Lords? Does the Book lay down that Communion once in three months or even once a month is sufficient? Does the Book say that a priest's office is a career, like the legal or medical profession, for making a livelihood? Does the Book permit churches to be shut up in gloomy silence all the week? What is the mind of the Book upon the ministry? What, according to the Book, are Baptism and the Lord's Supper? Let us be clear", said the Tractarians, "about membership in the Church of England, let us draw into the light of day not what we think about the Church but what the Church's Book has to say about itself and about us who claim to belong to it. Then the next step will follow. Are the truths enshrined in the Book of Common Prayer Catholic or Protestant? That is to say, have they always been the teaching of the Church or were they taken out of the Bible for the first time in the sixteenth century at the Reformation? Was there a period in history when the ministry was not threefold, a ministry of bishops, priests and deacons? When was the Holy Eucharist not celebrated every Sunday? Were the clergy, when the storms of the early persecutions ceased, expected never to be seen in their churches except on Sundays?

Then comes the further question. Is Church teaching as contained in the Book of Common Prayer really true in the sense that it is compatible with the mind of Christ and in agreement with Apostolic teaching so far as we can understand it from the pages of those books of the New Testament which have been preserved through the pious care of the Church".

Such questions as these came straight out of the Prayer Book considered as a handbook of the Christian faith. But there were others more practical and more concerned with the laity. For the Prayer Book is more a volume of praise and prayer, of sacramental rites and devotions, than a manual of Christian doctrine. Its main purpose is to bring men and women before the throne of grace and unite them in living, loving, confident communion with God through Christ. The Prayer Book taught the Tractarians to put religion before theology. It was to bring men to God that the Oxford leaders exalted the Holy Eucharist and taught the doctrine of the Real Presence. It was faith in Christ that caused them to repudiate the idea that Baptism could be no more than a pious and edifying ceremony. It was to make repentance deep and absolution a real remission of sin that Keble and Pusey revived the Prayer Book practice of private confession.

When the Movement began to work in village and town churches outside Oxford, other questions arose in the mind of every parish priest, "How am I to conduct this or that service? What dress am I to use in celebrating the Eucharist? What furnishings are needed for the Altar? What symbols of the

Christian religion may I set up in the Church?" The Church's Book gave little guidance on such relatively minor matters as these. Catholic tradition and practice must be the guide, checked, if need be, by St Paul's requirements that worship should be beautiful, orderly, edifying, intelligent and spiritual. In shallow minds these matters of ritual and ceremonial might be exaggerated out of all proportion to their worth, but the true successors of Keble and Pusey employed the externals of worship with the single aim of setting forth the glory of God and so helping souls to enter into communion with Him.

It is a gross misrepresentation of the Oxford Movement to describe it as preoccupied with matters which are belittled or despised under the opprobrious title of "ecclesiastical". Its leaders never forgot that the royal law has two sides, and if they were profoundly concerned with the things of God, they were no less deeply interested in the welfare of their neighbour. No men of their time, not even Maurice or Kingsley, toiled more unweariedly for the poor and oppressed than the early Tractarians. Nor did any social reformers work harder in the cause of ill-paid and overworked wage earners than their successors Canon Scott Holland, Bishop Gore, Father Stanton and Studdert Kennedy. It is worth noting here that the Social Service Board of the Scottish Church is at the present time responsible for two social undertakings which were the direct result of the Catholic revival in Scotland, the one a Home in Dundee founded sixty years ago by Bishop Forbes and the other a Rescue Home in Edinburgh carried on successfully by a Sisterhood which was founded as early as 1858.

The Oxford Movement began by appealing to scholars in Oxford and to men and women of culture elsewhere. But Pusey, for the church he built in 1845 at his own expense, chose not Mayfair, but a parish in Leeds with an Irish quarter living under appalling social conditions and ravaged in 1847 first by Irish fever and then by cholera. Ever since that time the heroes of the work of the Church among the masses of the people have been men like Prynne of Plymouth, Lowder of St Peter's, London Docks, Mackonochie and Stanton of St Alban's, Holborn, and Dolling of Portsmouth, all of whom drew their inspiration from the teaching of the Oxford leaders.

It must be confessed that in the work of missions overseas the influence of the Catholic revival was for a time much weaker, though Keble was an intimate friend of Bishop Gray of Capetown. But one by one the Universities' Mission to East Africa, the Oxford Mission to Calcutta, the Cowley Fathers' missions in India and Kaffraria provided fields for the missionary enthusiasm of the Movement.

Such was the way in which, from simple questions about the Church's profession, Creed, and practice, the Catholic revival awoke the clergy and impressed the people, brought interest and reality into worship, fanned the flame of missionary zeal both at home and abroad, and established institutions for the redress of social wrongs. Such a revival in its very nature is not an event but a movement which, once begun, cannot be said to end, for it is simply the work of the faithful seeking to make and keep the Church consistent with its own Creed and loyal to its own Master.

Did the great struggle which began in 1833 end in victory? If Keble were alive to-day he would see practically everything, for which he and his friends contended, firmly established in every part of the Anglican communion, and the larger part of his teaching regarded as incontrovertible. But if anyone ventured even to whisper the word victory his rebuke would be sure, "There is no victory for the Church militant. When Christians speak of victory they are sighing for a false peace and need the blast of a trumpet sounding a new advance".

There are not wanting to-day signs which suggest that the flame of enthusiasm which was kindled by the Oxford leaders has begun to die down. The catastrophe of the war was the death-blow of the Romantic movement in which the Catholic revival was born. We live in an age not of romance but of pessimism and disillusionment, when religion may once again become a dead habit or be taken merely for a useful adjunct to social life. A new revival will then be necessary. Its methods may differ greatly from that carried on by the great succession of Churchmen, from Keble on through Forbes and Mackonochie to Church, Liddon, Gore, Scott Holland and Studdert Kennedy. But its fundamental principles will be the same, consistency in truth, in devotion and in life.

CHAPTER II

# The First Stage

## 1833—1845

Spiritual movements within the Church are quickly forgotten; just because they are spiritual they find little or no mention in popular histories, which deal with crude facts and with human beings only in so far as these are linked with striking events.

Thus it is not altogether surprising to learn that the Oxford Movement at the present time suggests to some minds nothing more than the movement recently carried over to this country by the American Lutheran minister, Dr Buchman, which is sometimes known by the name of the Oxford Group. But the Oxford Movement known to history began a hundred years ago not in America but in Oxford University with men who were priests of the Church of England. Its first promoters, John Keble, Hurrell Froude, John Henry Newman, Edward Bouverie Pusey, Charles Marriott and Isaac Williams, were all Oxford men who had not only gained high academical distinction but had also occupied at least for some time official posts at the University. It was in Oxford that the Movement with almost Apostolic fervour sped to its first success. In Oxford it sustained its first defeat by the secession of Newman to Rome. From Oxford its disciples, after the bitter persecution which followed that disaster, were, like the first generation of Christians, "scattered abroad" carrying with them the seed of Catholic principle, not only to the great cities and country parishes of England, but also to Scotland and the colonies beyond the seas.

Primarily, the object was to save the Church of England from slavery to the State and from a deadening worldliness which had closed the eyes of its people to its own principles.

At the beginning of the nineteenth century the condition of the Church of England was pitiable indeed. It was execrated in many parts of the country as the enemy of the people. To the Chartists and the champions of the Reform Bill, bishops were worldly potentates whose chief business was to support the political party that had appointed them and to vote in the House of Lords against every reasonable measure of political reform. Lord Grey, the Prime Minister, had peremptorily told the bishops to set their house in order, and the Bristol mob had shewn their opinion of their bishop by setting his palace on fire. No wonder that the Church was unpopular. Many of the clergy were non-resident.[1] Not a few

[1] Out of 10,800 benefices, 6311 were without resident incumbents.

were pluralists who drew the stipends of three or four parishes and employed curates at £40 or £50 to conduct services. A priest who died as recently as 1865 held three livings and a canonry of Canterbury, his annual income from these sources being about £10,000. Another grave scandal was the sale of livings. What respect could the people of a parish entertain for their pastor when they knew that his appointment was due to a bid at an auction-sale in a lawyer's office? Once appointed it was almost impossible to eject a rector, however vicious his life might be.

In such conditions the standard of Church practice could not be other than wretchedly low. Communions were infrequent and the daily offices enjoined by the Prayer Book almost unknown save in cathedrals. The decencies of public worship were ignored. The furnishings of churches were in many cases inferior to those of a labourer's kitchen. In spite of the Catholic Creeds, the threefold ministry and the service book of the Church with its appointed Holy Days and Fast Days and its requirement of a weekly Eucharist, English religion had in large measure become petrified into a dreary and conventional form of Protestantism.

Yet even in this desert there were to be found here and there oases in which Christian graces and Church loyalties grew and flourished; so long as the Book of Common Prayer existed the truths and ideals of the Church could never utterly perish. The tradition of sturdy churchmanship proclaimed by the great Anglican divines of the seventeenth century and cherished in the eighteenth by men like Samuel Johnson and John Keble's father was still maintained and effectively proclaimed here and there by clergy like Dr Hook of Coventry, afterwards the famous Vicar of Leeds. Mr Gladstone who left Oxford before the Movement began used to say that he adopted the principles of the Oxford Movement simply by reading the occasional Offices in the Prayer Book; what he learned afterwards from Keble and Pusey merely confirmed his own discovery.

But the most signal proof of the latent power of Church ideals was seen when John Keble in 1827 published his first volume of poems under the title of *The Christian Year*. Here the teachings of the Church through the whole course of the Christian Year were invested with the imagination of a poet whose reverence and spiritual feeling were equalled only by that mark of the true Catholic, his deep love of the simple sights and sounds of nature. The book was received in thousands of homes as manna in the wilderness. It was hailed by competent critics as a masterpiece of devotional poetry. Principal Shairp of St Andrews, a lifelong Presbyterian who was a student at Oxford in 1841, perceived in *The Christian Year* "a tone of religious feeling deep and tender beyond what was common among religious men of the author's day, perhaps in any day". Our modern generation, to its great loss, has ceased to read *The Christian Year*, but as long as hymns are sung in Church, such poems of Keble as "New every Morning is the Love" and "Sun of my Soul" will never be forgotten. It is quite certain that *The Christian Year* would never have been read so widely in the early part of the nineteenth century, if there had not been in England much more real religion and loyalty to the Church than appeared on the surface.

Wordsworth and the Lake poets had prepared men's minds to look for the inward in the outward, the spiritual in the material, as Sir Walter Scott had taught them in his novels to look with a new interest and sympathy upon the romance of the past. Without Wordsworth, the poet of nature, and Scott, the poet and novelist of romance, *The Christian Year* could hardly have been written. So much that was directly religious did Keble see in the works of Scott that he dared to express the hope that the author of the *Lady of the Lake* might yet become the poet of the Church.

Thus the times were ripe for a new reformation. Wordsworth had supplied the philosophic ground by his insistence on nature as the vehicle of spirit, Scott had awakened the historic sense to the wonder of the past, Keble by his poems had created the spiritual atmosphere of humble confidence in God whose revelation through Christ sang in unison with the voices of nature and of the human conscience. Throughout the country, as well as in the University of Oxford, there were numbers of thoughtful people who only awaited a leader to give the signal for the battle which would end the slavery of the Church to the world and awaken her to the dignity of her mission.

In 1833 the leader appeared and the long fight for the liberty and the Catholic position of the Church began, strangely enough, with a sermon on July 14th in the University Church before a Judge of the Assize Court. On that day when John Keble entered the pulpit of St Mary's it seemed as if Providence had brought the ministers of State and Justice with all the paraphernalia of the law to be arraigned as before the judgment seat by a prophet of God. The title of Keble's sermon was "National Apostasy", and in effect it was a condemnation of the State as the main cause of the low estate into which the Church had fallen. Citizens, said Keble, would be loyal to the State as long as conscience allowed, but it behoved Churchmen to consider "how they might continue their communion with the Church established... without any taint of those Erastian principles on which she is avowedly to be governed". By a hundred years of subsequent history the preacher was justified in his conviction that the obstacle to Church progress in England was the intrusion of the State into spiritual affairs. From 1833 on to the rejection of the new Prayer Book by the House of Commons in 1929 the root cause of every crisis that arose in the Church of England may be traced to the Erastianism which treated the Church of Christ as the creature of the State. This is an aspect of the Oxford Movement which will commend itself to Scottish Presbyterians who have fought and completely won the battle for spiritual freedom.

So far as we know, the leaders of the Movement never met once for concerted action. Soon after the publication of Keble's sermon, a few kindred spirits met at Hadleigh Rectory, H. J. Rose, W. Palmer, A. P. Perceval and Hurrell Froude, the last named being the only Oxford representative present. At that meeting there was some talk of an association with its headquarters in London, but the idea was soon abandoned. It was, however, agreed that writing had to be done and this decision placed the Movement in the hands of the three Oxford men, Keble, his younger friend Hurrell Froude and Newman.

All three were young men, Keble being then forty-one, Newman thirty-two and Froude thirty. All three were men of the highest intellectual gifts. Easily first was Keble who, at the age of eighteen, had taken a double first at the University, a distinction only once gained before and that by Sir Robert Peel. Froude had been awarded a double second in 1824. Newman's scholarship, judged by academic tests, was inferior, for he took only second-class honours, though this failure was redeemed by his election to a fellowship at Oriel College in 1821. The Movement, though religious in motive, purpose and policy from the first, derived much of its driving force from the youthful energy and intellectual qualities of its first promoters.

To write tracts seems a tame enough occupation for gifted and high-spirited young men, but there are tracts and tracts. The small pamphlets, which came in rapid succession from their pens, at once set minds thinking which before assumed that the Christian religion required no thought. Not only dons in Oxford but also clerical households in many parishes were surprised to discover how interesting the Christian religion could be. There was no mistaking the deadly earnestness of their writers. The text prefixed to the first five volumes into which they were afterwards collected clearly indicates the temper in which they were written: "If the trumpet give an uncertain sound, who shall prepare himself for the battle?"

It was Newman who suggested this means of propaganda, and of the first twenty tracts he wrote nine. The first three tracts bear the date of

September 9th, 1833. Number 1 by Newman was addressed "To my brethren in the sacred ministry", and began "I am but one of yourselves, a Presbyter, lest I should take too much on myself by speaking in my own person". What, he urged, was the real ground on which their ministry rested? Was it on their successes or their temporal distinctions? "I fear", he wrote, "we have neglected the real ground on which our authority is built—our Apostolic descent." Yet this was the doctrine of the Ordination Service by which they were made ministers of Christ's Church.

These early tracts were intended to startle their readers. They were strong and even peremptory in tone, free from those qualifications which so often confuse the mind. They were not addressed to the many but to the few; the new reformation must begin with the clergy and the teachers. Yet they taught no "new thing". They called men to look back rather than forward; only by taking up its Apostolic position could the Church meet the dangers of the future or the flagrant abuses of the present.

In those days it was fashionable, as it is to-day in some quarters, to look upon the sacraments and rites and worship of the Church as "mere forms". The tracts called upon the clergy to treat the sacraments as divinely appointed means of grace, the services of the Church as the solemn approach of the people to the throne of grace, and rites and ceremonies as accessories of Holy Worship calling for seemliness and reverence in their discharge. By the year 1835 sixty-five tracts had been issued—a remarkable amount of published work for a period of less than two years.

In that year the Movement gained a recruit who in the words of Newman brought "a name and a standing and a personality to what without him was a sort of mob". This was Dr Pusey who though only a year older than Keble held the position of Professor of Hebrew and Canon of Christ Church. He had studied in Germany and counted among his friends great scholars like Schleiermacher, Tholuck and Ewald. "You may smile", said Mr Gladstone long after, "when I tell you that when I was at Oxford Newman was eyed with suspicion as a low churchman and Dr Pusey as leaning to rationalism." Pusey gave up the "Broad Church" position for much the same reasons that Newman abandoned the "Low". The eyes of both were opened to a new vision of the Church of England, and the awakening came partly from Keble and partly from the workings of their own minds upon the Book of Common Prayer and the history of the Church.

Pusey was a very different stamp of man from Newman. The narrow Evangelical upbringing of the latter led him to fierce invective against Rome.

Pusey could never have written as Newman did, "Popery must be destroyed; it can never be reformed". Newman was too eager for converts; in the eyes of some more eager for these than for truth. Pusey was for a revived and instructed Church. No sooner did he declare himself than he insisted that the semi-popular tract should stop. Christian truth must be proved and explained; better no converts at all than adherents devoid of well-founded convictions. So in 1835 the tracts became documented essays running to 300 pages. Pusey's tract on Baptism, signed with his initials, was "like the advance of a battery of heavy artillery where the battle had been hitherto carried on by skirmishes and musketry". His position in the University, his boundless charities, his deep humility and wide learning combined to make him one of the most prominent figures in the University. No wonder that very soon afterwards "the Tractarians" received the nickname of "Puseyites" from their opponents, for Pusey in virtue of his position and character had become in the eyes of the University the official leader of the revival.

No spiritual movement can go on for long without a spiritual atmosphere. The tracts themselves were the work of deeply religious men and carried their own spiritual flavour, but it was the sermons of Keble, Pusey and Newman that supplied the spiritual climate in which truth could strike root and grow. On all hands it is acknowledged that Newman's sermons created a great impression. A modern reader of the sermons may well wonder why, for in the printed page they are in no sense arresting or specially illuminating. Their power lies not in their originality or in the strength of their thought, but in the simplicity and beauty of their diction, in the solemn earnestness of their feeling, and in the practical and personal subjects of which they treated. The combined effects of tracts and sermons during the first few years of the Movement was to make religious questions in general, and the mission of the Church of England in particular, topics of deep interest in circles where before religion was the occasion for a jest or a jeer. Given another ten years of steady preaching and teaching, the Church of England might well have risen to the ideal of the Tractarians and become the soul of the nation.

But in 1838 a disastrous mistake was made by Newman in publishing the papers and letters of Hurrell Froude, the brother of the historian. Froude was one of those brilliant, audacious and lovable young men whose delight it is to shock people by railing at the commonly accepted ideas of the day. He was one of those dangerous persons who like to speak their mind regardless of consequences. In particular nothing pleased him better than, in speech and letters, to pillory the Reformation and make sport of the Reformers. He never could believe that Newman was serious in his opinion that Romanism was anti-Christian, and repeatedly declared that in some matters of faith and practice Rome was nearer the truth than the Church of England.

So long as views like this were confined to Oxford Common Rooms or to letters to friends no harm was done, but when Froude's remains were published after his untimely death in 1836, there was an outburst of indignation not only from opponents of the Movement but also from many who had been attracted to its teaching. The University rang with the "No Popery" cry, while in the country the Movement was denounced as a conspiracy against the Reformation. The Oxford Evangelicals as a counterblast set on foot a proposal to erect a memorial to three of the English Reformers, and in due time a pretentious monument with effigies of Cranmer, Ridley and Latimer was constructed on a prominent site in Oxford where these Reformers were certainly not burnt. From this time onward the Movement never succeeded in allaying the suspicion of Romanising, though nothing was further from the minds of Keble and Pusey than Rome, and though Cardinal Wiseman was as busy denouncing the Oxford Movement as was Dr Arnold of Rugby, who stigmatised its followers as "the Oxford Malignants".

But worse was to follow. The divided condition of the Church of England began to disturb Newman. He always denied, and rightly, that he and his supporters constituted a party in the Church. But in 1839 he began to wonder whether that was not all he could look for. Could the Church of England ever attain to a real Apostolic unity within itself? That was the question which disturbed his sensitive mind. "Our Church", he said, "is not at one with itself; there is no denying it." The attitude of the University authorities and of the bishops confirmed this belief. The heads of the University met the Movement simply with a mixture of contempt and dislike. The bishops went much further. One denounced the bad faith of those "who sit in the Reformers' seat and traduce the Reformation"; another described Tractarianism as "the work of Satan". The crowning test came in 1841 when Newman wrote Tract 90.

In this Newman set out to prove that the Thirty-nine Articles of Religion were as capable of a Catholic interpretation as the Prayer Book. This however was a much more difficult proposition than the Catholicity of the Prayer Book, for the Articles were the product of the sixteenth century in a sense that the Prayer Book was not. Nevertheless it was not difficult to shew that those Articles which dealt with Roman doctrine condemned not so much the official as the popular teaching of the Church of Rome. Few students would deny that, on the whole, Newman was right. But no sooner was the book published than it was condemned by the heads of colleges as evasive and dishonest. No attempt was made to meet the arguments of Tract 90 and no opportunity was given to the author to reply to the condemnation. Newman was straightway disowned by his own University, and in those days that was nearly as bad as to be branded as a heretic by his own Church. The bishops more timidly, but with equal unanimity, repudiated the tract. How Newman remained in the Church of England four years longer is difficult to understand and his famous *Apologia* fails to explain. Doubtless he hoped for better things from the authorities, but if so he was doomed to disappointment. For two years later Dr Pusey himself was suspended from preaching on account of a sermon upon absolution. It is strange to reflect that to-day neither Newman's tract nor Pusey's sermon would cause a ripple upon academic or ecclesiastical waters.

In 1845 Newman joined the Church of Rome. "I have", he wrote, "most honestly attempted to do a service to the Church of England and my tools have broken in the work." "The tools" of course were the formularies of the Church. But "the tools" had not broken. Keble, Pusey, Marriott, Isaac Williams and hundreds of others went on using the same tools, and for years proved them serviceable enough. How did they manage to remain loyal, when Newman deserted? They were faced with the same difficulties as he; they had read as much history as he. The fact is that Newman could not take his eyes off the power and prestige of Rome on the one hand and that of the English bishops and heads of colleges on the other; when the latter disowned him, the former seemed the only alternative.

The size of the Roman Church impressed him. The phrase of St Augustine (*securus judicat orbis terrarum*[1]), which first raised in his mind doubts of the Catholicity of the Church of England, was really an assertion of the power of Rome based on size. The world-wide sway of the Roman Church appeared to Newman almost a conclusive proof of the truth of Roman claims. But what is this but the argument from size—that truth is on the side of the biggest battalions? At the same time the English Church seemed to him to be discredited by the attitude of her bishops. Keble and Pusey and

[1] "The [Christian] world judges without fear of contradiction." Did Newman verify this quotation? The phrase, torn from its context, was misrepresented by Cardinal Wiseman and Newman and had nothing to do with the truth of the Roman position. Only by ignoring the Eastern churches could "The world" be identified with Rome.

the other writers of the tracts (for Newman was the only one who joined the Church of Rome) were convinced that the truth would prevail, though the officials of the Church for the time being might disown it. Keble, in the famous sermon that began the Movement, had prophesied that if the Church of England were true to its principles, victory would be sure. His prophecy has been fulfilled; and though for the Church militant there never can be victory in the sense that spiritual warfare will disappear, the fruits of the Movement he inaugurated are visible, as we shall see, in every part of the world to-day.

CHAPTER III

# The Second Stage

## 1845—1878

Newman's last sermon, preached on the eve of his secession, ended with this lament over the Church of England, "O my mother, whence is this unto thee that thou bearest children, yet darest not own them? Why hast thou not the skill to use their services nor the heart to rejoice in their love?" Pathetic words indeed! Yet how unworthy of the metaphor was his action! As if the ingratitude, coolness and want of skill in a mother could be an excuse for neglecting filial duty and leaving her. The very use of such a metaphor might well have given Newman pause. But the great preacher was not made of the stuff of an Athanasius who could dare to stand alone. Keble, Williams and Pusey were men of more resolute loyalty. The very coldness of their mother was a challenge to their love. Nevertheless the withdrawal of their friend was a heartbreaking experience. It seemed at first to cut the very ground from under their feet. What could they say to Romanists on the one hand and Protestants on the other? For now these two extremes enjoyed a common pleasure in the belief that the Catholic claims of the Church of England were devoid of substance. Were they right? Was the teaching of the past twelve years a piece of self-deception? What was the source of it? There was Scripture! Had Newman's secession changed the meaning of a word of Holy Writ? There was the Prayer Book! Had the Oxford leaders misinterpreted one of the most complete manuals of devotion and doctrine in the world? There were the three Creeds! Had these fled with Newman to Rome? There were the Thirty-nine Articles of Religion and the tradition of the great Anglican Divines from the Reformation with their appeal to Scripture and the primitive Church. Had these changed?

Dignitaries of the Church might repudiate Keble and Pusey as they had disowned Newman. What matter? Bishops and heads of colleges pass away along with their errors; truth would remain. Nothing had really changed. The ground was as firm as it had been when Keble blew his blast from the pulpit of the University Church on July 14th, 1833. Where God had set their feet, there they would abide unmoved by the storm of persecution and obloquy that now broke in full force upon them. Dr Brilioth in a recent work, *The Anglican Revival*, marked by a sympathy of insight unusual in one who is Swedish by birth and Lutheran in religion, declared that the Oxford Movement came to an end with Newman's secession.

Nothing could be further from the truth. Long before that disaster took place the principles of the Movement had spread far beyond the city of Oxford; it was known even in Scotland. But after 1845 it became clear that the larger field which was now penetrated and in part occupied demanded a change of operation from the academical to the popular. In fact the future of the Movement now lay with the clergy and laity throughout the land. Pusey and Keble were still regarded as leaders, but their friends and supporters were far more numerous outside Oxford than within it. Laymen of weight and position like W. E. Gladstone, Hope-Scott, Roundell Palmer, afterwards Lord Chancellor and Earl of Selborne, and Beresford Hope, were coming into prominence as strong sympathisers with its aims and ideals. Numbers of younger clergy as gifted as the original leaders of the Movement were gathering round Keble and Pusey, eager to carry on the work which had fallen from Newman's hands. Among these were R. W. Church, a master of English prose, A. W. Haddan, a scholar of distinction, and his brother who became first editor of *The Guardian*, A. P. Forbes, afterwards Bishop of Brechin, Henry Parry Liddon, known to history as perhaps the greatest preacher of his day, and many others. Christina Rossetti was beginning to exercise her poetic gifts and to shew the effects of the movement in her work. The first Anglican sisterhood was founded in 1845,[1] the beginning of a great army of women devoted to the service of Christ; Charlotte Young was already trying her hand at stories which carried Church ideas into houses of all classes of people. The Movement had gained a vitality which even Newman's secession failed to arrest; the leaders had done their part; the day of the smaller men had arrived. But now the supreme test had come. The truth and value of the Movement had to be proved in the common experience of the Church. The nickname "Poor Puseyites" which from 1845 began to be bandied about shewed that the stock of Tractarianism had fallen. The long record of blunders on the part of successive clergy at St Saviour's, Leeds (which had been built by Pusey), appeared to justify the epithet. Weak and unstable followers may discredit the work of the greatest saints and scholars; and the Oxford Movement, like all great causes, suffered much from misguided friends. Mistakes indeed were, under the circumstances, inevitable, for those clergy who sought to open the eyes of their people to the truth as they saw it had set themselves a tremendous task. The whole weight of officialdom was against them; public opinion was soaked with suspicion. They were marked men, regarded as

[1] The first Anglican sister, professed at Oxford in 1841, was Miss M. Hughes.

"dangerous" by their bishops, too dangerous sometimes to be trusted even with a curacy, much less a parish. John Keble remained a country parson at Hursley near Winchester to the end of his days, while clergy infinitely his inferior alike in character and ability moved on to canonries and bishoprics. Dean Church, described by Lord Morley as "the flower of English culture", would have been left buried in an obscure country parish, had not Mr Gladstone insisted on his appointment to the Deanery of St Paul's, London. Dr John Mason Neale, most versatile of men, nearly all his life was Warden of Sackville College (a semi-secular appointment), with a stipend of £28 a year. If such were the fate of the great, what could the average clergyman who sympathised with the Catholic revival expect but some poor curacy or a derelict church in a slum? Keble's own curate, Peter Young, was refused a licence on the ground of unsound views, and McMullen was denied the Oxford B.D. degree for a similar reason.

Meantime, the Catholic view of the Church took a somewhat different form in the University of Cambridge. Under the leadership of John Mason Neale, the Camden Society was formed in 1839, primarily to revive the study of Church architecture and worship. The promoters of this society were ecclesiologists rather than theologians. They assumed the Divine constitution of the Church and made it their business to advance the outward expression of worship by improving the buildings, the music, and the furnishings of the Church. This external aspect of the Catholic revival aroused little or no opposition, so long as its operations were confined to the restoration of churches. But in its publications it took the lead in explaining the ancient ornaments and furnishings required in liturgical worship, traces of which were to be found in every pre-Reformation church in the country.

Even if there had been no Camden Society, an interest in ceremonial was bound to follow a revival of Catholic doctrine. That this was needed no one could doubt. The worship of the Church had fallen miserably below St Paul's requirements of beauty, order and significance. Many of the directions of the Prayer Book had become almost a dead letter. The three-decker pulpit with clerk, reader and priest in ascending tiers dwarfed and obscured the Altar, which was commonly a mean-looking table covered with red velvet. The service was a duet between the priest and the clerk. For the sermon the preacher donned a black gown. To wear a surplice in the pulpit marked a preacher as a "Puseyite", and in Exeter, London and elsewhere caused riots. The revival of the special vestments for the Holy Communion which were enjoined in the Ornaments Rubric of the Prayer

Book, but had fallen into abeyance, excited the wildest resentment. The country seethed with excitement over coloured stoles, Altar lights, surpliced choirs and the like. The bishops gave orders, but had neither light nor reasoned guidance to offer. At last, after years of unsettlement, the Government was driven by the prevailing excitement to take legal measures to destroy this monster of ritualism, and Archbishop Tait was foolish enough to yield to the tumult. The result was the passing of the Public Worship Regulation Act of 1874, which was the occasion of Disraeli's cheap epigram about "the Mass in masquerade". The Act was of course defied, and a number of clergy were tried and sent to prison. There is nothing like martyrdom for spreading a cause, and when the martyrdom takes the form of imprisonment for conscience sake the advertisement is far-reaching. The ritualists in time became heroes, as indeed many of them were, Neale, Mackonochie, Lowder, Tooth, Enraght, whose lives were one long martyrdom of self-sacrifice and devotion.

Behind this contention about seeming trivialities stood Keble's old enemy, the Royal supremacy, now in the form of the Privy Council, now in that of Parliament, dictating to the clergy the methods of Divine worship. To Keble and Pusey matters of ritual and ceremonial were of small account; reverence and reality were all they sought. But the intrusion of State lawyers and members of Parliament into the realm of public worship at once brought them to the side of priests who were fighting not for stoles and chasubles but for the right of the Church to manage its own affairs. Keble in 1851 had stated his view of the relation of Church and State when he declared: "We are the only religious body in the Queen's dominions to which the following privileges are denied—(1) to declare our own doctrines, (2) to confirm, vary and repeal our own canons, (3) to have a voice in the nomination of our own pastors, (4) to grant or withhold our own Sacraments according to our proper rule as a religious body". He never lived to see those rights granted to the Church of England, but he saw the dawn of a new day of spiritual freedom in the Synod of Exeter in 1851 and in the revival of the Convocation of Canterbury in 1852. Pusey, who survived his friend by sixteen years, lived long enough to see the day breaking in the first Lambeth Conferences of 1867 and 1878 attended by bishops of Anglican Churches throughout the world, when it became possible to hope that contact with the non-established Churches of Ireland, Scotland, America and the Colonies would make plain the absurd restrictions under which the Church of England was condemned to carry on its work.

Here we must take leave of the Movement in

England and endeavour to trace its progress and influence in Scotland. But the reader should clearly understand that the Movement did not reach its full stride south of the Border till the ritual troubles were nearly over. He should think of the Movement in England spreading year by year in diocese after diocese, in parish after parish. In London fine churches like St Alban's, Holborn, St Paul's, Knightsbridge, St Matthias, Stoke Newington, were erected at great cost, each served by a staff of hard-working clergy. Great and stately churches of pre-Reformation date such as St Mary Redcliffe in Bristol and Leeds Parish Church were transformed into inspiring centres of spiritual activity, and village churches like Hawarden Parish Church (where Mr Gladstone regularly acted as reader of the Lessons), the parish church of Frome and many more shewed what could be done in small communities which heard the bell rung for frequent Eucharists and daily services, and saw their clergy going about day by day deeply concerned for the well-being of their people. No doubt mistakes were made by foolish clergy in many places, but these were as nothing compared with the interest which the Catholic revival aroused and the enthusiasm which it inspired in the souls of the people. A few figures may close this brief sketch of a remarkable epoch in the history of the Church of England. In the thirty years following 1840 over £25,000,000 was expended on church building or church restoration; in the thirty years after 1884 more than £38,000,000 was given for the same purposes. In London alone 240 churches were built in fifty years with districts assigned them and endowments provided.

The question when did the Oxford Movement end admits of no answer. It certainly did not end with the cessation of the tracts and the secession of Newman. Had Pusey been asked the question he would have said that, as it had no precise beginning, so it could have no dated end; it was a revival, not an organisation; its principles were the principles of the Church, not those of a party, and its task was to open blind eyes to their reality and power. In this sense the Oxford Movement is as truly alive to-day as it ever was.

CHAPTER IV

# Beginnings and the first Public School in Scotland

## 1833—1857

"The ancient but poor and suffering Episcopal Church." So did Sir Walter Scott rightly describe the Church with which, though by birth a Presbyterian, he dared to ally himself from early manhood to the end of his life. There was no question as to the poverty of the Church. In Scott's early days it was reduced—to quote his own memorable phrase—to "the shadow of a shade". Disestablished in 1689, its fortunes had gone from bad to worse owing to the sympathy of its members with the Stuart kings and their taking a hand in the risings of '15 and '45. Following the defeat of Prince Charlie the Church was subjected to the persecution of severe penal laws for nearly fifty years; and during that troublous period its ministers often had nothing better than a kitchen in which to conduct in secret Sunday services and other ministrations. When its cup of suffering was full, only four bishops and forty-two priests remained where one hundred years before fourteen bishops and archbishops and a thousand priests had ministered.

The rigours of imprisonment and banishment were abolished in 1792, but the clergy of the Episcopal Church were still debarred by statute from officiating for a single day in the Church of England till 1840. At that time they numbered no more than eighty-nine including six bishops and even this small body was not wholly united; for those in the south were for the most part "qualified" clergy, in English or Irish orders, while those north of the Tay were hereditary Episcopalians deeply attached to the Scottish Liturgy, which at that time was little known in the south of Scotland.

Bishop Walker of Edinburgh and Bishop Russell of Glasgow, themselves deeply imbued with the Scottish non-juring traditions of the eighteenth century, had done much to bring together the two types of Churchmanship. Nevertheless it would not be untrue to describe the northern clergy as "high" and the southern as "moderate" or even "low".

In the north both clergy and laity were by conviction and sympathy Tractarians long before the *Tracts for the Times* were written. They had retained the use of the Scottish liturgy and the practices accompanying it. To the Churchmanship of the north the Oxford Movement could contribute nothing in the shape of Christian doctrine. The teaching of the Oxford leaders had already been expressed by Bishop Jolly in his catechism of 1829 and in his work on the Christian Sacrifice of 1831. In such Catholic truths and practices as the Divine origin of the Church, the Apostolic succession and constitution of the ministry, Baptismal regeneration, the Real Presence and the Godward offering of the Eucharist, the Communion of Saints and Prayers for the Departed, the Reservation of the consecrated elements for the sick, reverence for the appointed fasts and festivals of the Church, the north was at one with the Tractarians long before their names had reached Scotland.

In the south the emphasis was different. There both clergy and laity were more "English" and less Catholic. Though most of the "qualified" chapels by the year 1833 had been absorbed into the Scottish Episcopal Church, their traditions still savoured of their English origin. The Scottish Communion Office contained meat which was too strong for their spiritual constitution, nor did they hesitate to express their preference for the milder milk of the English rite. Their Churchmanship was of a more colourless type. They shrank from obtruding points of difference with their Presbyterian brethren.

The prevailing Calvinism of Scotland was at this time becoming distasteful to numbers of educated Presbyterians, and the services of the

Book of Common Prayer to not a few of them were a welcome change from the dreariness of Presbyterian worship. As a consequence the Church in Edinburgh was growing dangerously popular. It was "genteel" and almost fashionable in some circles to belong to the Episcopal Church. Nothing was more likely to imperil this popularity than to lend countenance to doctrines that might raise among these the "no Popery" cry. The policy of the south, therefore, was to preach a somewhat harmless Gospel and to win cultured people through the quiet beauty of the Prayer Book services. Not unnaturally the clergy made much of the connection with the Church of England and paid much deference to the English bishops. The argument from size drew the southern clergy to the Church of England as it drew Newman to Rome. It was some relief to their sense of inferiority as members of a small disestablished Church to claim union with the powerful Church of England south of the border.

Anything calculated to create the impression that the Scottish Episcopal Church differed from the Church of England was studiously avoided. It was, therefore, natural that the Oxford Movement should for some time be regarded with suspicion, especially in the dioceses of Edinburgh and Glasgow, simply because it was not under the patronage of the official leaders of the Church. Only after the

Movement had established itself in the Church of England did Scottish Church people south of the Tay welcome the teaching and preaching of the Movement, and even then in a number of congregations the tendency was to be content with minor improvements in public worship and to leave the weightier matters of doctrine and practice to a few congregations of a more adventurous type. It is a fair statement of the position to say that the aesthetic element in the Movement was cautiously and gradually accepted in the south and resisted in the north, whereas the south was slower to assimilate the teaching of Keble and Pusey to which the north had been long accustomed. Improvement in the outward form of worship attracted the south, the Church principles of the Tractarians gained the sympathy of the north. And although the two sections have now come together, it is still possible to perceive here and there signs which shew that this difference in emphasis has not even yet been wholly obliterated.

As early as 1833 the Scottish bishops, especially Jolly, had welcomed the movement but the real pioneers were young laymen of position. Most of them had been students at Oxford, and there had caught a new enthusiasm for the Church by reading the *Tracts for the Times* and a high ideal of Christian life and duty by listening to the sermons of Newman in the University Church. Some of these young men were personal friends of Keble, Newman and Pusey, the saint, the preacher and the scholar of the Movement. Prominent among these was W. E. Gladstone, drawn to the teaching of the Oxford leaders because, like them, he was convinced by his own study that the prevailing beliefs and practices of Church people were inconsistent with their own Prayer Book. James Hope-Scott, a friend of Gladstone, then at the height of his career at the English Bar, was another, whose devotion to the Church had become such that to the dismay of his parents he begged to be excused from attending the services of the Established Church—an almost unpardonable offence in those days. A third was the Hon. G. F. Boyle, afterwards Earl of Glasgow, and a fourth, Lord Forbes.

But the distinction of being the first to bring the Oxford Movement and its leaders within the public notice of the Scottish people belongs to a woman, the young Marchioness of Lothian, who after her marriage came to settle in Newbattle. She had become interested in the Tractarians through her brother, Mr John Talbot, and her brother-in-law, Lord Henry Kerr, both of whom were at Oxford when she came to Scotland. In 1839 she was reading Tract 72 on Prayer for the Dead and studying the devotional writings of Keble's friend, the poet Isaac Williams. The romance of religion went to her head. She thought nothing of walking from Newbattle to Dalkeith for an early Celebration. She travelled to Leeds to see Dr Hook and afterwards kept up a lengthy correspondence with him. In London she attended the services at Margaret St Chapel (afterwards, All Saints, Margaret Street), then the centre of the Movement there. Her ardent spirit was not attracted by what she saw of the cautious ways of the Scottish Episcopal Church and she knew little or nothing of its history; though Newbattle might at least have reminded her of the saintly Bishop Leighton. There was no Episcopal Church nearer her home than Dalkeith, where the Duke of Buccleuch had a private chapel. With the duchess she formed an intimate friendship and, in a letter of 1842, remarks that "the poor little Duchess is an object of suspicion in her family as I am in mine". It was not easy in those days to take one's religion seriously or to practise it with any enthusiasm.

When these two young women began the practice of Communion every Sunday before breakfast, the marchioness walking all the way from Newbattle, they were regarded as rather mad. In 1840 the marchioness moved from Newbattle to her estate in Monteviot near Jedburgh, the nearest Episcopal Church being at Kelso, ten miles away, which at that time was the only church in the south of Scotland except Haddington. Too consistent and independent to adopt the usual expedient of being Anglican in England and Presbyterian in Scotland, she determined to erect a church in Jedburgh in which the teaching and services should follow the principles and ideals of the Oxford Movement.

Her enthusiasm apparently had drawn from the Bishop of Glasgow some cautious warning as to the dangers of Puseyism, for in one of her letters she makes the caustic remark that "the Bishop was Puseyite enough" (speaking of the accommodation of the new Church) "to use the word kneelings for sittings". Plans for the new church were prepared by Butterfield, one of the most distinguished architects in England, and in 1841 the foundation stone was laid by the marchioness. Two years later the church was consecrated and to this service four of the leading Tractarians, Keble, Hook, Dodsworth and R. J. Wilberforce, were invited. The sermons preached by them on August 15th, 16th and 18th, 1843, were published in 1845 in a small volume. These sermons have an old-fashioned ring about them, but they are both attractive and effective because definite and well-directed pleas for loyalty to the ideals of the Church as expressed in the Prayer Book. There runs through all the sermons one great idea, that the best way to ensure depth and reality in the religious life is the Catholic way of frequent

Communion, daily services, and open churches. "The services of God's Church", said Keble, "are so many breathing places through which the light and air and fragrance of Paradise and of Heaven may find for a time some way into our prison, refreshing our languid senses, and preparing them gradually for that which would be otherwise too much for them to bear." It was a great week for the Scottish Church, for the erection of St John's, Jedburgh, was quickly followed by new churches at Kelso, Hawick, Melrose and Selkirk, all of which owed much to the munificence of the Duke of Buccleuch. It was, no doubt, a great week also for the marchioness but as events proved it came too late. The marchioness had ploughed her lonely furrow too long and events in England produced an unsettling effect upon her mind. In 1845 she hears that rumours of Newman's approaching defection are widespread, and writes "I cannot believe about Pusey". But in 1850 when the Privy Council laid down what might be taught in the Church of England about Baptism and when Manning and others in consequence seceded to Rome, she declared, "Manning's course shall decide mine. I have said to myself I would not move as long as he did not and now he is gone, I am miserable". So simple and easy was the passage to Rome in those days! In later days a favourite but strange (though not new) argument with the marchioness for the claims of Rome was this: "the Roman Church claims to be infallible. Have we any such certainty for the Church of England? Therefore, it seems, that the safest place is the Church of Rome".

The tragedy of this story, however, lies in the fact that it was to the English Church and not to the Scottish that the marchioness looked for guidance, and that Manning carried more weight with her than all the Scottish bishops. It was an ominous beginning for the Oxford Movement in Scotland. Nevertheless St John's, Jedburgh, went quietly on with its daily services and its weekly Communions, though sadly weakened by the fact that its foundress, living only a mile away, no longer entered its door. St John's, Jedburgh, in the simplicity of its architectural style and in the perfect finish of every part of it, recalls the very spirit of Keble, modest, reverent and above all thorough in the loving care bestowed upon every detail of screen, pulpit, bench ends and even tiles. The church will go down to history as the only Scottish church in which John Keble ever officiated. Nor will it be forgotten in the future that two of its communicants, the Marquis of Lothian, Secretary of State for Scotland 1887–1892, who did not follow in the steps of his mother, and Mr Bertram Talbot, grand-nephew of the foundress, devoted their great gifts of administration for many years in loyal service to the Church of their baptism.

The first congregation in Edinburgh to welcome the ideals of the Oxford Movement was Old St Paul's, where the Rev. John Alexander restored the Scottish Liturgy, introduced the "choral service" and even dared to decorate the church at Easter. But violent opposition caused Mr Alexander to resign in 1846, and accept the charge of the new church of St Columba, carrying with him a considerable part of his old congregation. Old St Paul's made no progress for forty years, when under the leadership of the Rev R. Mitchell-Innes, and after him, of Canon Laurie, it became the great church it now is. St Columba's Church for many years was the only church in Edinburgh which openly followed the teaching of the Tractarians, but when the Forbes family left Edinburgh for the country, its fortunes declined.

In 1841 there was issued by the six Scottish bishops a letter addressed "to all faithful members of the Reformed Catholic Church"—a phrase that caused an elevation of eyebrows in some quarters—appealing for funds to erect and endow a building which should be at once a theological college for the training of clergy and a public school, on the English model, for the education of boys. The credit for initiating this scheme belongs not to the bishops but to two laymen of Tractarian sympathies, W. E. Gladstone and Hope-Scott. They were joined by Dean Ramsay of Edinburgh, and had little difficulty in persuading the bishops of the wisdom of the proposal. Upon so daring an enterprise the bishops of their own accord would hardly have ventured in days when the Church was so poverty-stricken that the stipends of its clergy in some cases amounted to less than £80 a year. It was the Oxford Movement rather than the Scottish Church that produced Glenalmond. That statement is best proved by the fact that A. C. Tait (afterwards Archbishop of Canterbury) surprised his friends, who in his biographer's words, "had failed to realise the strength of his Churchmanship", by becoming a prominent subscriber to the fund. Tait, in a letter to Bishop Terrot of Edinburgh in 1842, expresses the fear lest the scheme should fall into the hands of "what is now very generally regarded amongst moderate men as a dangerous and revolutionary party who are striving to break down the barriers which separate us from Rome in her fallen state". No description of the aims of the Oxford Movement could be more unjust. Doubtless Tait was right in his view that the origin, the driving force and much of the financial support of the scheme came from men who had caught from Oxford their enthusiasm for the Church. But it was not Mr Gladstone's intention, still less that of Dean Ramsay, to found a college and public school for the furtherance of any party principles. The aim was to establish a college in which the future clergy of the Church should be prepared for the sacred ministry and boys could receive a liberal education based on Church principles and carried on in a Church atmosphere. Money poured in steadily, and in less than two years the foundation stone was laid. The Rev. Charles Wordsworth (afterwards Bishop) was on Mr Gladstone's suggestion appointed warden and the school was ready for occupation in 1845, Lord Lothian entering as its first pupil. By this time Newman's secession had taken place and the majority of the Scottish bishops, alarmed by this event and fearing that the college might suffer from its connection with the Catholic revival, did their utmost to exclude the Scottish Communion Office from the college services. Mr Gladstone strenuously resisted this proposal and ultimately secured a compromise by which it was agreed to use the Scottish and English forms of service on alternate Sundays.

The college had not been in existence more than three years when the "no Popery" cry was raised against its management. The complaints were entirely groundless, and the warden took strong measures to vindicate himself against the stupid charges laid against his administration of the school. That a man of Wordsworth's extremely moderate views should be accused of Romanising shews the narrow and intolerant temper of the time. In view of it we can hardly be surprised at the zeal with which the majority of the Scottish bishops strove to identify themselves more and more with the Church of England "as by law established" and so clear themselves of any complicity with the Oxford Movement.

As a theological college, Trinity College, Glenalmond, was a failure, because it proved impossible to combine the education of boys with that of young men. But as a public school it became a great success, though like all public institutions it never won the cheap success which is the worst kind of failure. It was the first school in Scotland established on the lines of the great English public schools.

The buildings were designed by Henderson in the Gothic style of architecture revived by the Oxford Movement, and their size and beauty embody a faith and courage and generosity marvellous for those days when the Church was only beginning to recover from the prolonged persecution and destitution of the past. But Churchmen like Mr Gladstone and the Hon. G. F. Boyle, and families like those of Buccleuch and Lothian were not the persons to offer to God that which cost them little.

This is not the place for a history of Glenalmond.

But two incidents must be briefly noted, one to shew that in Scotland as in England persecution was the lot of those who took their stand on Catholic principles, the other to indicate the low estate of a disestablished Church in the 'fifties. William Bright came to Glenalmond as tutor in 1848 with a brilliant reputation from Oxford. A born scholar and a man of singular charm, he was probably the most effective member of the staff. But it was not easy to keep on good terms with the authorities and at the same time adhere to definite Church principles. Bright was too good a scholar to have any leanings towards Rome. He was never more than a sober Churchman like Keble and Pusey. Nevertheless the warden, Dr Hannah, and a majority of the bishops accomplished his dismissal in 1859, the result being that Oxford University gained a professor of ecclesiastical history and Glenalmond lost its most brilliant teacher. Bright's name is familiar throughout the world as the author of the Communion hymn "And now, O Father, mindful of the Love", and it also stands high among historians of the nineteenth century.

The second incident also concerns an historian, G. F. Browne, who in his early days served on the staff of Trinity College, Glenalmond, and afterwards became Bishop of Bristol. When Browne came to Glenalmond in 1857 he desired to be ordained by a Scottish bishop. But Wordsworth, who knew the ways of the world better than most, pointed out to his young colleague that Scottish Orders might be a bar to his advancement if he returned to England. Accordingly Browne, contrary to all precedent, was ordained by Bishop Wilberforce of Oxford who, at Wordsworth's request, consented to waive the legal formality of a title. It was only when the Clerical Disabilities Act was passed in 1864 and the Scottish clergy were placed on an equality with English clergymen, that the stigma attaching to Scottish Orders was removed.

A word must be added to credit the diocese of St Andrews with the foundation of the first Girls' Boarding School in Scotland in 1851. St Margaret's School was due chiefly to the enterprise of the Rev. A. Lendrum, a fervent supporter of the Oxford Movement. For several years it was most successful but on his departure to England was allowed to disappear.

CHAPTER V

# Two young Cathedral Builders

Lasting enthusiasm needs to be fed from two streams, the one a deep conviction of the mind, the other a steady emotion of the heart. Of this kind was the enthusiasm of two young Scotsmen who were at Oxford in 1847, Lord Forbes, resident at Oriel where memories of Keble and Newman were still fresh and vivid, and the Hon. G. F. Boyle, undergraduate at Christ Church where Pusey could be seen and heard every day. To these two young men, the latter twenty-two, the former eighteen years of age, belongs the credit of erecting in Perth the first cathedral in Scotland and, with the exception of St Paul's, London, the first built in Britain since the Reformation. To formulate the idea of such an undertaking would be comparatively simple even for young men, but to persuade older and wiser men that the scheme was feasible was a very different thing. These young Scotsmen, however, were fired with the enthusiasm which can think and plan as well as feel.

Their first step was to secure the consent of the bishop of the diocese who lived in Peterhead, and the next to win the support of Mr Gladstone for the scheme. They were successful in both. The fact that Trinity College, Glenalmond, had only just been opened and still needed funds for its completion would certainly have made cautious persons hold their hands for a time. But young men are proverbially in a hurry, and Lord Forbes and G. F. Boyle were not to be kept back by counsels of delay. Wordsworth, Warden of Glenalmond, regarded the scheme as a mad affair; it would withdraw financial support from Glenalmond. Others opposed it because its champions were Puseyites, and others again because in their view the opening of a large church was not justified by the handful of Church people then resident in Perth. Undismayed by the powerful arguments of their elders, the two friends, backed by steady encouragement from Oxford, determined to go ahead. A strong committee was formed. Mr Gladstone joined it, and money began to flow in quickly, till it amounted to the sum of £6000. In 1848 Mr Butterfield was appointed architect, and in the following year the foundation stone was laid by Bishop Forbes of Brechin, acting for Bishop Torry who was too infirm to attend. In 1850 the new cathedral, consisting of the choir and one bay of the nave with accommodation for 350 people, was consecrated under the patronage of St Ninian on December 11th, 1850. The sermon was preached by Dr Neale, whose friend, the Rev. T. Helmore, well known as a pioneer of ancient plainsong music, sang the Litany. It was on this occasion that Dr Neale received the only offer of ecclesiastical dignity that came to him during his whole life, the deanery of the new Scottish cathedral. Had he been able to accept this appointment, the Scottish Church would have gained immensely by the accession of a man of his gifts, but the world of historical and liturgical scholarship would probably have been the poorer. For his own peace of mind Dr Neale was well out of the deanery of St Ninian's Cathedral which was destined to a long period of trouble and strife that would have blasted the hopes of men less sanguine than Lord Forbes and G. F. Boyle.

A cathedral chapter was set up, statutes were framed and the services and ceremonial of the new church were arranged in consultation with George H. Forbes, Neale and others. The ritual included lights, vestments, unleavened bread and apparently incense, curiously enough the black gown was worn in preaching at the afternoon service, probably in imitation of English University churches.

In 1852 Bishop Wordsworth was elected Bishop of St Andrews, and then trouble began. The bishop was too ambitious a man either to appreciate the principles of the Oxford Movement or to sympathise with its spirit, though he had known Keble and Manning in his early days. To the surprise of Mr Gladstone who was instrumental in bringing him to Scotland, he took up the position of "use and wont" and, as bishop, set his face like a flint against the ceremonial which, in deference to the bishop, had been already considerably reduced from the original standard. In 1856 the bishop withdrew his sanction even of the eastward position at Holy Communion and at last placed the cathedral under his episcopal displeasure by refusing to have anything to do with it for nearly thirty years. To this the only response of Mr Boyle, now Earl of Glasgow, was to raise his subscription from £200 to £600 in 1869. The passage of time had not abated the enthusiasm of the two Scotsmen who built the cathedral and, though subjected for years to the bitter disappointment of seeming failure, both lived long enough to see the cathedral become a power in the diocese; had they survived till 1930 they would have found the hundred communicants of 1853 grown to a thousand.

One might have thought that to take a hand in the erection of a great school like Glenalmond and a lead in the establishment of a new cathedral would have sufficed to satisfy the enthusiasm of the most ardent. But these two projects only fired the zeal of Boyle for more. In the same year in which the foundation stone of St Ninian's, Perth, was laid, he founded and endowed a collegiate church, with a college attached to it, in the Island of Cumbrae on a site adjacent to a residence of his own called "The Garrison".

The spirit of the founder as well as the objects of his benefaction are best described in his own words from the Preamble to the Constitution dated 1853 when Mr Boyle had reached the age of twenty-eight,

> In the Name of the Father and of the Son and of the Holy Ghost, in one glorious and undivided Trinity, Three Persons and one God, I, George Frederick Boyle, considering how blessed a work it is to rear a Temple to the Most High God, wherein His praises may be duly celebrated, His Sacraments administered, and His Holy Word preached; and considering also the spiritual necessities of this Church and Diocese, and how needful it is that Priests, Deacons and other Ministers of the Church should be maintained and educated, who may constantly offer unto Him the sacrifice of praise and make known unto men the unsearchable riches of Christ, have caused to be erected a collegiate church with a college attached to it, which I have offered and dedicated to the Third Person of the Ever Blessed Trinity under the name of "the Church and College of the Holy Spirit", with the constitution following; and have, moreover, provided an endowment for the Provost and Canons who shall serve the aforesaid Church, aid the Bishop of the Diocese in feeding the flock committed to his care, and train in sound religion and useful learning such students and scholars as may be resident within the College or its precincts.

A collegiate church was an entirely new thing in Scotland. In a sense it was a revival of the Augustinian Order of Canons adapted to modern conditions. The intention was to attach a body of clergy consisting of a provost and at least four priests to the collegiate church, two of whom should be responsible for the full round of services required by the Prayer Book, and two who should be at the disposal of the bishop for missionary purposes in the diocese. Evidently what was nearest to the heart of the founder was the erection of a church in which Catholic worship should be offered, not with the omissions dictated by expediency, but with the completeness required by the Church in its own Prayer Book. The youthful founder, however, was well aware that if the clergy had no more to do than to conduct the full services of the Church day by day, they would inevitably degenerate to the level of the "mass priests" of the Middle Ages. So there was added, as the Preamble to the Constitution shews, the work of education and the work of missions to the Divine work of worship.

This fine ideal of a community of clergy and laity living together in an atmosphere of prayer, sacred learning, and missionary interest, bound together by the invisible ties of faith and charity, was crowned by the provision of a home within the college for a number of aged and infirm clergy who might "seek to spend the close of their life in the worship and service of Almighty God and in preparing to render an account of their stewardship". The church and college of Cumbrae were intended to be a monastery in spirit and in purpose, free from the restrictions and rigorisms of ancient monasticism and satisfied with the standard of worship and devotion implied in the Book of Common Prayer. In fact it was an attempt, bold and remarkable for the times, to practise what the Oxford leaders taught.

The foundation stone of the buildings was laid on May 29th, 1849, and the church was opened on Whitsunday 1851. The south wing of the college, the canons' house, was ready for occupation in November 1850, and the north wing for the accommodation of young men preparing for the English Universities was completed in October 1851. How much money was expended on the buildings will probably never be accurately known. What is certain is that their erection and endowment greatly impoverished their benefactor who contributed for endowment alone a capital sum of about £10,000; the church and the two wings of the college must have cost at least £20,000 more. Yet the Earl of Glasgow, as he afterwards became, never regretted an enterprise which was regarded by many at the time as rash and even quixotic in its lavish munificence.

The college was one of the greatest interests of G. F. Boyle's life, and when he persuaded John Gibson Cazenove to join its staff as canon and vice-provost in 1854 he had the satisfaction of seeing his ideals faithfully carried into practice for more than twenty years. The *College Calendar* of 1877 gives the names of the residents from the year 1849 onwards and, if we take 1874 as representative, we find in residence four canons, nine English clergy, an assistant tutor (F. E. Warren, the distinguished liturgical scholar) and twenty-two students, most of them Oxford and Cambridge men who spent their vacations at Cumbrae, and seven choristers. The number of theological students in residence that year was six.

From this it will appear that the college in Cumbrae had become a serious rival to the official theological college in Glenalmond, which was under the direct supervision of the Scottish bishops. Led by Wordsworth the bishops were eager to "anglify" the Scottish Church and in pursuit of this policy they had deposed the Scottish Liturgy from its position of primary authority in the Church in 1863. As they had frowned upon the new cathedral at Perth for many years so they viewed the college of Cumbrae with undisguised suspicion and created throughout the Church the impression that it was a separatist institution.

Not a word of encouragement or even of appreciation did the Earl of Glasgow receive save from his own diocese, which passed a resolution of appreciation in 1874 when the collegiate church became the cathedral of the Isles. In the 'eighties some of the objects of the foundation had to be abandoned for financial reasons, and the college lost much of its prestige, its very existence being at one time imperilled. For a considerable time it pursued a languishing career until 1917 when the Very Rev. R. O. P. Taylor became provost and restored its reputation. Under the present provost, the Very Rev. Claude O'Flaherty, it has come back again to its kingdom; and its work in stimulating thought and devotion among the clergy and laity is recognised and appreciated on all hands.

No buildings in Scotland speak more eloquently of the Tractarians than the fine church and college of Cumbrae. The college indeed might be part of an Oxford college, transported to the little island that looks out upon the hills of Arran and Ailsa Craig. Modest, shy, retiring it seems to recall Keble himself; in cloisters, refectory and libraries there is a quiet charm that recalls the sweet attractiveness of the author of *The Christian Year*, while the whole range of buildings, including the church with its lofty spire, suggests the confident security with which the influence of the Movement inspired the whole Church. The interior of the church is dignified and impressively significant; one would not wish to remove a fragment even of the somewhat bizarre tile decoration of the walls, every detail of which has its Christian meaning and reflects the spirit of the period. Four of the windows are the gift of the founder to the memory of his revered master, John Keble, and doubtless it was the founder's suggestion which resulted in the offer of an honorary canonry to him. Bishop Wordsworth declares that Keble told him he accepted this honour, the only distinction he ever received from the Anglican Church, with the idea at the back of his mind that if he were driven out of the Church of England he would find a refuge in Scotland within the college in Cumbrae. Curiously enough, W. E. Gladstone, the great Liberal statesman, had a somewhat similar design in view; for his friend, G. E. W. Russell, says that in his early days Gladstone was prepared, if the Church of England were proved anti-Catholic, to go, not to Rome, but to the Episcopal Church in Scotland. Fortunately, by the year 1860, Catholic principles had made good their place in the Church of England and neither Keble nor Gladstone were driven to the extremity of leaving the Church of their baptism.

The founder of Cumbrae College and Collegiate Church succeeded to the title of Earl of Glasgow in

1869 and died in 1890. No son of the Scottish Church has ever treated his spiritual mother with more open-handed generosity than he. It would be pleasant to record that his work and worth were fully appreciated. But this ardent layman met the fate of most of God's pioneers. Benefactors as a rule get little thanks for their gifts, especially when the gifts are unusually generous; the founder of Cumbrae received none save on the one occasion we have mentioned. The Scottish bishops of the time were not big enough to encourage ventures that ran away from the cautious calculations of ecclesiastical polity. The truth is that the founder of Cumbrae lived fifty years before his time. He had a vision of an institution something like Mirfield thirty years before Bishop Gore thought of such a thing. It is sad to reflect that the sudden fall in the price of land, combined with his benefactions to the Church and to charitable institutions, reduced the founder of Cumbrae to real poverty. For years he had lived quietly in "The Garrison" with his mother that he might build the church and college, and long after it was completed he had to suffer misfortune approaching financial ruin.

Strong and convinced Churchman though he was he never lost the respect of his own people in the west, though his political opponents did not scruple to employ religious prejudice when he stood as a Parliamentary candidate for Bute. During the election of 1865 abuse of every kind was flung at his religious principles, but from Boyle's lips there fell not one word of recrimination or even of complaint. His own supporters, doubtless, had little sympathy with his Church principles, but such was their admiration of his fairness, toleration and high ideals that they returned him as their member.

CHAPTER VI

# A Scottish Pusey

In the year 1840, at the age of twenty-three, there went up to Oxford a Scotsman of birth and parts, Alexander Penrose Forbes. His father was a Scottish judge, Lord Medwyn by title, a deeply religious man who, when his sons were boys at Edinburgh Academy, wrote a letter urging them to regular attendance at Holy Communion as the most important religious habit in life. His uncle was Sir William Forbes, whose name appears in Sir Walter Scott's *Marmion* as the intimate friend of the poet and novelist. One of his ancestors, Lord Pitsligo, had the distinction of being "out" in the risings both of 1715 and 1745. Thus, with Jacobite blood in his veins, the Romantic Movement in his mind and religion mediated by the Church and Sacraments of Christ in his heart, Forbes was the very man to be attracted by the teaching of the Tractarians.

Oxford was a second choice with him; for at the age of eighteen Forbes had gone out to India in the service of the East India Company. A serious breakdown in health, which left his constitution weak all his life, brought him home for good in

1839, resolved to dedicate himself to the ministry of the Church. When he entered Brasenose College in the following year, Newman had already lost heart in the Movement, and shaken by the increasing disapproval of the heads of colleges was thinking of resigning St Mary's and retiring to the village of Littlemore. It was Pusey, therefore, not Newman who became Forbes's hero. Pusey believed in the Church of England and therefore never despaired of the Movement. Forbes took the same line; he had learned long before he came to Oxford to believe the Church to be Catholic as well as Reformed. Newman, on the other hand, brought up as an Evangelical, appeared to Forbes to believe in the Movement as long as it succeeded, rather than in the Church of England in which he served. Forbes never could treat any movement for the revival of forgotten truths either as a symbol of the Church itself or as a test of Catholicity proved by its success. His occasional meetings with Newman never came to anything and they ceased when Forbes left Oxford.

With Pusey, on the other hand, Forbes felt at home from the first. He admired the wide range of his learning which strengthened and enlarged his own Churchmanship. But it was the saint in Pusey more than the scholar that brought him constantly to Tom Quad and Christ Church. In the deep humility, the calm sincerity, and the patient practice of communion with God which were as characteristic of the Oxford professor as his learning, Forbes found an unfailing source of inspiration. Here was religion in a life, not in a book. The intimacy that grew up between the two became in time as close as that between a father and son. It was from Pusey that Forbes took the gravity, the quiet seriousness and the abiding sense of the Divine which became so natural in him that some of his contemporaries in Scotland said he was never seen to smile and others that he had no sense of humour.

No doubt Forbes looked serious. All his portraits represent him as at least ten years older than he was, his face, seamed with lines of suffering even in early manhood, surmounted by a massive head of black curling hair hanging over a forehead in which under heavy eyebrows were set penetrating dark eyes. In stature he was tall and erect and when he spoke his voice was unusually melodious. Pusey in his letters remarks, as many others did, upon his brilliant conversational ability and his high intellectual gifts. But Forbes kept these endowments in the background to such an extent that only a few in Scotland ever saw in him a scholar and man of the world as well as a saint; so completely had he learned from Pusey to subordinate his natural gifts to spiritual interests. But by nature Forbes was far from being the sad man he looked. His letters from Oxford to his brother George are those of a playful, high-spirited young man with a keen sense of humour. Take this extract as a specimen written to his brother in his curate days: "Sing tooralooroo! I wish you had been down here to-day, the weather is so fine; you would have enjoyed it so much. I suppose in Scotland you never see blessed Phoebus except through a mist as thick as the froth on a pot of porter. Why do the Puseyites dislike pews so much in churches? Do you give it up? Because they are so much attached to forms". And his later letters to the same brother abound in shrewd humorous touches and Scotch phrases, which shew that the painters and photographers of Forbes missed something when they depicted his face as almost impassive and sad in its gravity.

His friendship with Pusey was strengthened during his diaconate to which he was ordained in 1844 for the curacy of St Peter's, Oxford. He came to the ministry four years later than the average ordinand, with a wide knowledge of life and affairs, and it was no surprise to his friends when Pusey invited him to go to Leeds in 1847 and try to clear up the mess which hot-headed young clergy had created at St Saviour's. There he lived alone in the vicarage, working single-handed a large and difficult slum parish. His health suffered severely, especially when the deadly Irish fever came to the town, and he had to spend long days in the hospitals which were crowded with the sick and dying.

In the previous year, a request had come from Stonehaven, a small fishing village on the Kincardineshire coast, to take charge of the Scottish Episcopal Church there, and by the advice of Dr Pusey he had accepted this obscure incumbency. His arrival in Scotland was opportune, for in August 1847 the diocese of Brechin was without a bishop. W. E. Gladstone, who used to boast that every drop of blood in his veins was Scottish, was at that time on a visit to his father, Sir John Gladstone of Fasque. The talk turned on the episcopal vacancy. "Why not Forbes?" said Gladstone. "He is thirty-two, a son of one of the finest Churchmen in Scotland, a man of great gifts, with a reputation vouched for by the best minds in Oxford." Gladstone interviewed the dean and some of the clergy and soon persuaded them that Forbes was the man. A few weeks later he was elected by a large majority and on the Feast of St Simon and St Jude 1847 consecrated Bishop of Brechin. In those days the Church was so poor that the only way in which a Scottish bishop could live was by assuming the pastoral charge of a congregation. This had become the usual thing and, though Forbes possessed ample private means and wished to devote himself to the work of a bishop alone, he found it impossible to break this bad tradition. Accordingly he held the dual office of Bishop of Brechin and incumbent of St Paul's, Dundee, to the end of his life.

St Paul's was the only Episcopal church in Dundee at that time. Its place of worship was a dingy "chapel" up a stair in Castle Street, provided with the meanest of furnishings and destitute of any symbols of the Christian faith; the services were of course those of the Prayer Book but the black gown with bands was the vesture of the preacher.

The congregation was as dull as the chapel, and two years' work in Dundee reduced the bishop well-nigh to despair: "I am doing no earthly good here", he wrote to his brother in 1849. "The people seem dead and the necessity of attending to the diocese interrupts any steady work, while I feel I don't do half the work in the country I might do if more at leisure and yet with our democratic constitution I dare not give up Dundee. We should have a split."

The religious atmosphere of Scotland after the disruption of 1843 was hot with prejudice, ignorance and violent controversy. By the great majority of Presbyterians the bishop was regarded as an arch-Papist and the label of Papist in those days was rather worse than that of heathen. Among some of his own people Bishop Forbes's sacramental teaching was viewed with suspicion.

So persistent were the attacks made upon him both from without and from within that the Vestry of St Paul's drew up and sent to the bishop a warm expression of their appreciation of his teaching and of his self-sacrificing devotion to his people. The bishop's reply is of interest as a good example of his literary style as well as a revelation of his own mind and heart.

Dundee December 9th, 1850. To The Lay Members of the Vestry of St Paul's.

In returning you my sincere thanks for the kind expressions of your goodwill and confidence, I must begin by disavowing, from the bottom of my heart, any right to those flattering terms in which you allude to my pastoral labours among you.

I am most grateful to you for your words of sympathy, in referring to the annoyances which have been the occasion of your letter. They do not move me much as regards myself. I regret them on account of our poorer brethren, who are apt to be misled by them. "They know not what they do" who wantonly attempt to sow dissension between the clergy and their flocks.

You do me more than justice in what you say of the nature of my teaching. It has been always my desire to hand down safely the faith "once delivered to the saints" as contained in the Holy Scripture, and as defined by our own Church in her offices, articles, and canons, and through her by those documents of the Primitive Church, to which she herself refers us.

I have ever endeavoured to direct your thoughts to the practical truths of our Holy Religion; and, while

I do no tundervalue the all importance of a correct faith, I have ever endeavoured to avoid adding to the unhealthy religious excitement of these days by the angry invective of polemical controversy.

As a general principle, I am unwilling to bring a "railing accusation" against those who differ from us, or to encourage the use of unauthorised tests of opinion; but I gladly assure you of my warm attachment to that Branch of Christ's Holy Church, in which, by God's providence, I have been called to preside, an attachment which I have again and again expressed by taking the Oath of Supremacy, and by signing the XXXIX articles and the canons of the Episcopal Church.

Every association of family and early training, solemn vows and engrossing duties, the recollections of the past and the hopes of the future, bind me to her; and though I may mourn over the lukewarmness and coldness of some of her children, and be anxious for her safety in these days of sifting and trial, I am not without good hope that He, who brought her through the troubles of the last century, will not abandon her in this.

The assurance of your prayers has been a strength to me, and the expression of your affection and sympathy, a comfort, in the many cares and sorrows of the Episcopate, and in the anxieties of declining health.

As for my enemies, secret or open, known or unknown, I freely forgive them all.

That Almighty God, the Father, Son, and Holy Ghost, may bless and keep you, is the earnest prayer and benediction of, Your faithful servant in Christ, Alexander, Bishop of Brechin.

This letter marks the beginning of a new epoch in the bishop's life; the people of Dundee now began to take the bishop to their heart. In the new atmosphere of peace and appreciation he was able to carry on preparations for the erection of a new church to take the place of the poor chapel which his congregation had outgrown in more than one sense. The year 1853 saw the church of St Paul's completed from designs by Sir Gilbert Scott, a remarkable achievement for those days of small things. Now, one would think, was the time for a complete break with the bald simplicity of the services conducted in the old chapel. But that was not the bishop's way. When the congregation entered their fine new church, the services went on just as before. There was more music. The Altar was more dignified but there was nothing on it save an alms-dish. It had a new frontal but, like the old one, it was of red velvet with no more than a cross embroidered on it. The bishop believed, as the old non-jurors from Bishop Rattray to Bishop Jolly, that the Catholic faith might be kept whole and undefiled, though the Eucharist was said and not sung, though there were no vestments, no Altar lights nor even a brass cross on the Holy Table. With the bishop the principle was people first and things second. It was his fortune not to live long enough to see the external openly employed to express the spiritual.

This seems to be the place to repudiate a legend about the bishop's preaching which originated from a sketch of his life written by the Rev. T. I. Ball who, for a short time, was curate at St Paul's. In this the writer, who notoriously was more ingeniously clever than accurate, suggests that Bishop Forbes concealed his principles and preached vague platitudes to please his old-fashioned flock. Such an insinuation is absurd in view of what has been already said. One wonders if the curate listened to his Bishop's sermons; certainly he could not have read a small volume of them, entitled "Are you being converted?" or he would never have written his rather superior criticism. The bishop was an impressive preacher, perfectly simple and clear, whose sole aim was to bring his rather dull and unintelligent hearers to God. One shivers to think what he must have suffered from his self-assertive curate.

No man can be Catholic at heart and dull to the cries of the poor and needy. The bishop was deeply concerned in the physical welfare of people whose conditions of labour were as unhealthy as the hovels in which they were condemned to eat and sleep. His charity to the poor was unbounded and he was often imposed upon by rogues. "Bishop," said one of his clergy, "that man to whom you gave a shilling is a humbug." "If I were as poor as that man," retorted the bishop,

"I should be a humbug too." He was known to take blankets off his own bed, wrap them up in a parcel and carry them to a starving woman left destitute by a drunken husband. These were times when poverty was only a handbreadth from starvation, and disease and dirt brought the rate of mortality to a height unknown to-day in the worst slums of our great cities. In the late summer of 1871 cholera raged in Dundee, and the bishop was in the thick of it, never waiting to be summoned but going in and out constantly among the plague-stricken people, mounting crazy stairs to the garrets in which the sick lay dying on beds that would in our day be deemed too foul for dogs.

Nor did the bishop confine himself to private ministrations and personal charities. He took up his pen and in letter after letter sought to arouse the public conscience to pressing questions of public health. It was by his energy that a Rescue Home for Girls was established as well as an Orphanage and a Convalescent Home.

And all this time, unknown to people of the diocese and even to most of the clergy, the bishop was undertaking a number of tasks that would have kept most men active if they had been doing nothing else. Two of these call for a brief comment:

(1) The bishop was a scholar all his life. During the twenty-five years of his episcopate there was not a month in which he was not engaged in some

work for the press. As early as 1849 he was preparing a manual of intercession for his people and his Companion to the Altar and Catechism had a large circulation.[1] Now to write devotional works is from the public point of view equivalent to committing intellectual suicide. Just as both Keble and Pusey in the latter period of their lives were credited with little or no intellectual gifts, because the one wrote religious poetry and the other works of devotion, so Bishop Forbes, because he used his pen to help the average Christian to practise his religion, gained a reputation for saintliness which eclipsed his distinction as a scholar. His principal interests lay in the rarely trodden fields of liturgy and hagiology, and his work on the Arbuthnot Missal and on the Kalendar of Scottish Saints cost him years of labour. The former owed much to his brother who was a genius in interpreting ancient liturgies, the latter was the fruit of his own unaided study. The bishop also wrote on doctrinal subjects, and his books on the Nicene Creed and the Thirty-nine Articles passed through more than one edition. The last named, published in 1867, owed much to Dr Pusey, who not only supplemented and tested the

[1] Forbes also edited the Remains of A. W. Haddan, as well as the Lives of St Kentigern and St Ninian. Besides writing many devotional works he translated Arvisenet's *Memoriale Sacerdotalis Vitae*.

patristic references but also revised considerable sections of the work. In fact it would hardly be too much to say that there is nearly as much of Pusey as of Forbes in the book. There can be no doubt that this work was intended, at least in part, as a contribution to Christian unity, and especially to such a unity as might be acceptable to the Roman Catholic Church. If, however, the official doctrines of the Church of England as expressed in the Thirty-nine Articles were no more than anti-Roman declarations, any efforts towards reconciliation or even towards outward peace were vain. Bishop Forbes's book is a careful examination of the Articles to prove that even the most anti-Papal of them repudiates not so much the official teaching of the Roman Church as the mediaeval corruptions associated with the Mass, Purgatory, Penance and the Invocation of Saints. The work in fact was a treatise dealing at length with the very subject which Newman had attempted more briefly in Tract 90.

(2) For twenty years Pusey and Forbes patiently entertained the forlorn hope of reunion with that Roman section of Christendom with which the Church of England had been for many centuries in complete communion. Their view was that if both Churches would rid themselves of prejudice, a real unity without rigid uniformity might be achieved. On the one hand there was an intelligent doctrine of the Mass as well as a crude popular one, and on

the other hand there was a positive and Catholic conception of the Eucharist in the Church of England as well as a cold and narrowly Protestant one. Both Churches might come nearer one another by conforming to their own standards and rejecting the popular interpretations both of the Council of Trent and the Thirty-nine Articles.

All this appears reasonable enough; but Pusey and Forbes had stronger grounds for their hopes than theories of this kind. There were not a few Roman Catholics on the Continent, especially in France, who encouraged their efforts and kindled their hopes. We must remember that in the 'fifties and 'sixties the Roman Church was much more liberal, because much less ultramontane, than it is to-day. Indeed to many in France the Infallibility Dogma of 1870 came as a surprise and a shock; even Newman was not prepared for it. But when this new doctrine was promulgated, Pusey and Forbes knew that all hope of any union with Rome was gone, although there were Roman Catholics who still believed it possible in 1890 (when Lord Halifax secured a hearing), and even in 1924 when the Archbishop of Canterbury's deputation met Cardinal Mercier's at Malines. All the efforts in the end were frustrated by the opposition of the English Roman Catholic hierarchy instigated by the all-powerful Jesuits both in England and in Rome.

Like all other leaders of the Oxford Movement Forbes had to pay the price of his devotion to the cause of liberating Christian doctrine and worship from the limitations of popular Protestantism. The cause of the bishop's long martyrdom was a Charge delivered to his clergy on the Eucharist. It was natural that the bishop should follow Keble and Pusey in endeavouring to make explicit the significance and value of the Sacrament of the Altar. In 1855 Pusey had published his work on the Real Presence and two years later, Keble wrote his treatise *On Eucharistic Adoration.* In the same year an ecclesiastical court set up by the Archbishop of Canterbury had condemned Archdeacon Denison for teaching the doctrine of the Real Presence and Eucharistic Sacrifice. Echoes of this controversy were heard all over Scotland, and Forbes determined to make a full statement upon the subject. The Charge was published in the following year, and its publication threw all the other Scottish bishops into a state of panic; they saw in the bishop's Charge a challenge to the decisions recently pronounced by the archbishop's court.

Three of the Scottish bishops put out a document repudiating the conclusions of Bishop Forbes. It was a hasty and ill-conceived statement and committed the bishops in advance to a policy of prolonged persecution, which inflicted so deep a wound upon the bishop's sensitive spirit that he carried its scar in his heart to the end of his life. Keble in virtue of his Scottish canonry wrote a long letter to the Bishop of Edinburgh dealing respectfully not with the Charge but with the narrow and trite paper issued by the bishops.

In the following year Bishop Wordsworth carried the matter much further by persuading the six Scottish bishops to sign a letter censuring the bishop's Charge by reason of its "tendency to undermine the great foundations upon which our formularies rest", a phrase thoroughly characteristic of Wordsworth's mode of thought. Keble again came to his friend's rescue and issued a criticism of this foolish and provocative letter. He had little difficulty in shewing that if there were dangerous tendencies in Forbes's teaching, these were nothing to the dangers involved in accepting the teaching of the Scottish bishops as stated in their letter.

It is unnecessary to follow the controversy further: suffice it to say that when Bishop Forbes was formally put on his trial for false teaching in 1859, his judges were bishops who had already condemned him unheard. Keble stood by his friend throughout the long trial; Pusey did not appear, fearing that his presence would do more harm than good. By this time, however, Bishop Wordsworth, whom Forbes described as "one whose bitter animosity has grown into a fanaticism, of which the bent is to put me and those who think with me down", was now thoroughly alarmed at the train of consequences he had started and the verdict, instead of being a demand to retract, tailed off into a mild admonition.

Few reasonable Churchmen to-day would deny the statement that in the Eucharist the Real Presence of Christ is given to His people and that the element of sacrifice or offering cannot be excluded from the Eucharist. Difficulties, however, arise as soon as we begin to express in words these many-sided truths. Possibly the bishop carried definition and exposition too far. At any rate his brother George could not agree with the language of the bishop's Charge. Bishop Forbes in a later Charge was able to clear up some misconceptions of his teaching, and there can be no doubt that his firm stand for the high and Catholic conception of the Eucharist gave a new impetus, if not a new direction, to the teaching of the clergy on this great mystery of the faith.

It was no small encouragement to the bishop during this galling experience, when he was practically ostracised by his brother bishops for three years, that he received a warm-hearted address signed by 5386 working men, thanking him for all that he had done in Dundee for themselves and their children and concluding with the wish, so natural in Scotsmen who love "a bonnie fechter", that he would "triumph over his adversaries".

It would take a volume to describe the amazing output of work during the last fifteen years of his life. Let it be enough to say that he left five large churches in the town of Dundee where, on his arrival in 1847, there had been only one poor upstairs chapel, that he saw at least five churches built in the country where there had been either none at all or insignificant chapels, that the clergy of the diocese increased to twenty-one and the communicants in Dundee alone rose from three hundred to two thousand.

During the period from 1847 till the close of 1874, the bishop could be seen once, twice or thrice a year making his way across Tom Quad to Dr Pusey's lodgings in Christ Church, Oxford. An old friend of the writer, then an undergraduate at Christ Church in the early 'seventies, used to describe the tall figure of Bishop Forbes with stooping shoulders and grave, lined face, the face as of one who had been wounded in the house of his friends; he looked an old man. Yet when he died in 1875, "the most universally mourned bishop in Scotland since the Reformation", he had not completed his fifty-ninth year.

## CHAPTER VII

# Some Fruits of the Revival

## 1860—1880

In the year 1860 the "English Church Union" was founded, and the Oxford Movement from that date onwards lost to some extent its spontaneity by coming under the guidance of a definite organisation and in some degree under the direction of a committee and officials. The Union was initiated at a conference of sixteen laymen under the chairmanship of Sir Stephen Glynn, a relative of Mr Gladstone. Its objects were defensive rather than propagandist, and were so framed as to make membership possible for all who were prepared to maintain the doctrine and discipline of the Church of England, and to help clergy or laity suffering from unjust treatment in spiritual matters.

Pusey became a member of the Union on the ground that some such organisation was necessary to defend persecuted clergy, but he took no prominent part in its affairs. Like many others he regretted a step which, in his view, was bound to convey to unthinking people the impression that Catholic principles were the peculiarity of a party rather than the privilege of the whole Church.

Five years later the Protestant party replied by setting up the "Church Association and National Protestant League". Thus the party system rooted itself in the Church of England; the English Church Union standing for Catholicism, the Church Association vociferous for the Reformation and more recently the "Modern Churchmen's Union" claiming to uphold "modernism" or "liberal" views. It is all a little puzzling to the outsider and, probably, has more effect than the wildest ritualism in driving weak brethren over to Rome.

In the year 1865 the Scottish Church Union was established on the same lines as the English; fortunately the two other English societies have no representatives in Scotland. When organisations of this kind are set up, it is natural for their members to look upon those who are reluctant to join them as moderate, if not colourless, in their convictions. But few members of the English Church Union south of the Border and none in the Scottish Union would regard themselves as the only champions of Catholic truth and the sole representatives of the teaching which Keble, Pusey and Forbes revived in England and Scotland, and for which they suffered harsh and bitter persecution.

The fact is that, by the year 1860, the principles of the Tractarians had lodged themselves more or less firmly in the minds of so large a body of the clergy and laity that the movement spread by the momentum of its own truth and the example of its own adherents. No organisation could arrest nor could any Union or committee greatly quicken its progress.

In the Scottish Church, while the bishops were cultivating closer relations with the Church of England, the teaching of the Tractarians was quietly penetrating into every church and congregation in the land. It is somewhat amusing to reflect that in the 'sixties and even in the 'seventies and 'eighties a choral service, an Altar cross, coloured stoles and harvest decorations were the chief outward signs of Scottish "Puseyism", while clergy who dared to place candlesticks on the Altar were "advanced", those going so far as to light the candles being reckoned more advanced still. In only a few churches were the ancient Eucharistic vestments used: St Ninian's Cathedral, Perth, St Margaret's, Aberdeen, and All Saints, Edinburgh, leading in the establishment of a practice which is now almost universal in cathedrals and quite common in other churches.

As we have seen, Bishop Forbes knew none of these things. He even went the length of forbidding them, on one occasion ordering one of his clergy to return to the donor a pair of candlesticks which had been presented for the Altar. The bishop deemed it more Catholic to obey the Prayer Book by celebrating the Holy Eucharist every Sunday and Holy Day and by reciting Mattins and Evensong every day than to introduce symbols of the faith for which at that time the people were not prepared. In his diocese there were few churches in which the daily offices were not said. Indeed it may be said that the recitation of the Daily Services, the observance of Saints' and Holy Days and the early Sunday Eucharist were regarded by thinking people as the true notes of Churchmanship. The externals of worship were very simple. In the 'eighties a Scotsman might firmly believe in Apostolic Succession and the highest doctrine of the Eucharist and yet refuse to go to church the moment Altar lights were introduced. This attitude of hostility to changes in the externals of worship was not the result of blind conservatism but, in many cases, was due to mistaken zeal for reality and reverence in worship. It was only as symbols became significant and the aesthetic sense of the Scottish people developed that ritual and ceremonial were accepted as helps to worship and devotion.

The period 1860–1880 was one of rapid, almost dangerously rapid, progress in the extension of the Scottish Episcopal Church. Every year saw new churches erected, all of them in the Gothic style of architecture which had come with the Catholic revival; the ceremonial of the ancient Church might be unpopular but its architecture was the only style in which decent churches could be built. The early English style, dear to the Tractarians for its simplicity and modesty, was most commonly adopted, though the more dignified Perpendicular appealed to the cultured taste of Bishop Forbes when he was considering plans for St Paul's, Dundee.

The awakening of the Church by the influence of the Oxford Movement resulted in a widespread desire in Scotland to provide every diocese with the Catholic equipment of a cathedral church to hold the bishop's "stool" or, as modern usage has it, the Episcopal throne. In 1866 a new cathedral was erected in Inverness for the Diocese of Moray, Ross and Caithness, a wonderful achievement for one of the smallest dioceses in Scotland. The Diocese of Edinburgh followed in 1879 with St Mary's, designed by Sir Gilbert Scott, then the largest cathedral in Britain built since the Reformation except St Paul's, London. The building was erected by the munificence of two Scottish ladies, Mary and Barbara Walker. St Mary's, Glasgow, also of Scott's design, was erected in 1871, and for long was regarded as the bishop's church, though it was not formally declared a cathedral until 1907. St Paul's, Dundee, a finer example of Scott's genius than St Mary's, Glasgow, was literally Bishop Forbes's church for more than twenty years, but only became a cathedral in 1905. Aberdeen had in St Andrew's a bishop's church and this, though a poor building in spite of Sir Robert Lorimer's improvements, was accepted as the cathedral of the diocese in 1913. Thus every Scottish diocese possesses a cathedral church, with a provost and a chapter of canons. But it cannot be said that the cathedral system has been worked with greater efficiency in Scotland than in England.

On October 17th, 1866, Archbishop Longley laid the foundation of the new cathedral in Inverness. This was a daring thing to do, for royalty did not look kindly on disestablished churches in those days. In an address the archbishop boldly declared that he was "animated by a desire for union and communion with the Scottish Episcopal Church, the only true representative of the Church of England in Scotland". Presbyterians were indignant and Erastians in England denounced this official recognition of Scottish Episcopacy. *The Times* on the following day came out with a leader which began with the following sentence, "The Archbishop of Canterbury has appeared in the capacity of a dissenter". The prejudice which would turn the accident of national establishment into an article of faith died hard. Only two years before—and then mainly owing to the support of that tried friend of the

Scottish Church, Mr Gladstone, and men of position and enlightenment like the Duke of Buccleuch—the last stigma which debarred priests in Scottish Orders from official position in England was wiped out. The utterance of *The Times* shewed that Keble's old enemy, Erastianism, was not yet dead. English archbishops and even English bishops had to be careful in their public dealings with the disestablished Episcopal Church.

It took several Lambeth Conferences to put "establishment" in its place; strangely enough the first Lambeth Conference in 1867 owed much to Archbishop Tait, then Bishop of London, the last of the "Church and State" bishops, who got the shock of his life when his "liberal" friend, Dean Stanley, on that occasion refused the use of Westminster Abbey for a service in which Scottish, American and Colonial bishops were to communicate together! At the last Lambeth Conference in 1930 the bishops of the Provinces of Canterbury and York were outnumbered by the bishops of "non-established" provinces by nearly ten to one. In such conditions establishment cannot count for much.

One happy feature of the Catholic revival in Scotland may be illustrated best by an anecdote. Some years ago a Scottish priest was asked by his junior, an Englishman, whether he might observe the Festival of Corpus Christi in a college chapel. "No," was the reply, "that festival does not occur in our Kalendar." "Oh," said the Englishman, "I thought we were more free in matters of worship in Scotland than in England." "Yes," came the answer, "the Church is more free and consequently the individual is not." In Scotland the Church moves as a whole constitutionally; in the Church of England, owing to its want of freedom, the lead has to be taken by individuals, as was done by John Keble in 1833 and by Bishop King in 1887. The small measure of freedom obtained by the Act of 1919 which set up the National Assembly of the Church of England leaves the Church far from being mistress in her own household even in spiritual affairs. On the other hand the Scottish Church at the beginning of the nineteenth century dreaded to exercise its own liberty. Good, saintly bishops like Jolly and Torry refused again and again to countenance, much less encourage, the meeting of a General Synod. Even in 1899 foolish fears of hasty or disruptive legislation still lingered; and though these had disappeared by 1910 there were not a few even then who urged the exclusion of certain necessary changes in the Prayer Book until the Church of England made a move forward. That cautious policy would find few advocates to-day. The Scottish Prayer Book of 1929 has raised the level of Churchmanship in a remarkable degree, though at the same time it avoids rigidity and assigns a generous liberty both to the clergy and their people. The result is an absence of "extremes", a sensible attitude to minor points of ceremonial and harmonious co-operation among all the Scottish clergy.

One of the first acts of Bishop Forbes was to follow his master, Dr Pusey, in securing a place in his diocese for the work of women under the life-long vows of poverty, chastity and obedience. In 1855 he instituted the community of St Mary and St Modwenna to carry on work on the practical lines of visiting and nursing among the poor people of Dundee, though this Sisterhood had no consecrated chapel till 1871. In 1858 the Community of St Andrew of Scotland in Edinburgh and later on the Sisterhoods of St Margaret and of the House of Bethany were established in Aberdeen. Scotswomen contemplating such a vocation have as a rule sought admission to the larger English communities, but it must be acknowledged that vocation to the religious life in Scotland has been much more rare an experience than in England. The work of Sisters during the last fifty or sixty years is the direct result of the Oxford Movement. Their value to the Church, however, is known only to the few, who are privileged to catch glimpses of these "Spouses of the Church" carrying out their pious and charitable duties so quietly that their very existence is unknown to the great majority of Church people.

In conclusion a word may be added on the growth of those gatherings known as Retreats which also were the direct outcome of the Catholic revival. One of the first objects of the *Tracts for the Times* was to awaken the clergy to a sense of their own need of spiritual discipline and deepening. Bishop Forbes and a few other clergy occasionally used to attend a Retreat at Chislehurst, Kent, conducted by that great saint, Father Benson, Superior of the Society of St John's, Cowley. In Scotland Retreats were for some time suspected as dark conspiracies for spreading "Puseyism", whereas they were simply prayer meetings with addresses and meditations for the deepening of the spiritual life.

Even as late as 1881 many of the clergy were afraid of them. In that year we find Provost Noyes of Cumbrae writing to the canons as cautiously as this:

I should be glad if you would kindly favour me with your opinion on the propriety of permitting a Retreat to be held within the walls of the College. Some years ago the question came before the Chapter and it was not at the time considered expedient to grant the permission then requested. But the whole subject of Retreats has been so fully ventilated since then, and they have been found by experience to be so conducive to the advancement of the spiritual life of the clergy, that they have been, under one form or another, adopted by various schools of thought within the

Church. A Retreat can no longer be regarded as a Badge of Party. Under these circumstances I have thought that the time has arrived when the question may fairly be reopened.

Should the replies which I may receive be favourable to the project, I propose that a Retreat especially intended for the clergy of the West of Scotland should be held in the College during the Autumn Vacation under the conduct of some able and earnest man of moderate views, should I be fortunate enough to secure the services of such a one.

It was not till the 'nineties that Retreats became at all common even for clergy, though Father Benson and others not infrequently conducted Retreats at St Margaret's, Aberdeen. Now there is not a diocese in Scotland in which the value of Retreats is not recognised both by clergy and laity.

CHAPTER VIII

# The Catholic Revival and the Scottish Prayer Book[1]

In the first stage of the Oxford Movement liturgical interest was weak. Newman knew little about ancient forms of worship, though at one time he contemplated an English adaptation of the Breviary. Pusey's interests lay in the fields of doctrine. Keble was familiar with eastern liturgies and was a strong admirer of the Scottish liturgy, but he had no first-hand knowledge of the subject. In fact liturgical study had scarcely begun. William Palmer was the only one of the Oxford leaders who was deeply interested in those forms of worship by means of which the Church in ancient times guided her people to the throne of Grace. His *Origines Liturgicae* was published in the year before the Movement began, but the book was too learned and too dry a work to influence more than a comparatively few.

Though the appeal of the Tractarians to the Book of Common Prayer was both consistent and

[1] Detailed information on this subject will be found in *The Scottish Prayer Book, its Value and History*, by W. Perry, D.D. (Cambridge University Press, 1929).

emphatic, the idea of proving its Catholicity by comparing its services with ancient forms occurred to few. Fewer still ever thought of tracing mediaeval services to their sources. One might have expected that those who were attracted to Rome would make some study of Roman service books, but there is no evidence that Newman, Ward or Manning possessed any real knowledge of the Roman service of the Mass till, as Roman Catholics, they learned how to use it. It is remarkable that while the authority of the Church of Rome appealed to men of philosophic temper like Newman, its devotional spirit to saintly men like Faber, and its efficient organisation to practical minds like Manning, not one person with any grasp of liturgical principles left the Church of England for that of Rome from 1833 to 1932. For indeed there is no cure for "Roman fever" so effective as the study of ancient forms of worship, especially when the study includes Roman service books themselves.

It was unfortunate that liturgical interest was a late and not an early result of the Oxford Movement. John Mason Neale was one of the first to take up this study seriously about 1850, and from that time onward there has been a succession of liturgical scholars in the Church of England, increasing in numbers in the 'seventies and 'eighties, the equals if not the superiors of any in the Roman

Catholic Church. Had the liturgical revival appeared earlier, seceders to Rome would have been fewer.

In Scotland both Bishop Forbes and his brother George were keenly interested in the subject from different angles. The latter was pronouncedly Scottish, Eastern and anti-Roman; the former English, Western and sympathetic with the Roman Catholic devotional system. On their death the lamp of liturgical learning burned low, till Bishop Dowden poured into it the rich oil of first-hand knowledge and placed under its clear light the many imperfections of the Prayer Book of 1662.

When the work of revising the Scottish Prayer Book began in 1918 the Scottish tradition was still strong, though influences from the south had come in to modify and enrich it, these being in the main Western or Roman. The revision completed in 1929 was Catholic in the best and widest sense of the word, though the practical aim of rendering the services of the Church profitable to the people was more prominent than any other.

Indeed it is impossible to distinguish the practical from the Catholic, for in the course of the revision it was found again and again that Catholic elements in worship were the most practically useful. Thus, shortened forms of confession and absolution were introduced as sensible alternatives to the long Reformation forms, though the fact that they had been used for centuries in the Western Church reinforced the practical argument. So, too, the revival of the "Invitatories" to the Venite had their practical value in emphasising the teaching of the Church seasons, though here also the repairing of a link broken at the Reformation had an appeal of its own.

Again, the introduction of an Eastern form of litany, as a short alternative to Cranmer's, created a new bond with the great liturgies of the fifth century on which the Scottish liturgy had been modelled. The ancient practice of prefixing biddings and appropriate versicles and responses to intercessions, was a return to pre-Reformation usage. The services of Holy Communion, Baptism, Confirmation and Ordination were all enriched in different ways by drawing upon the liturgical wealth of the ancient Church. Some may dismiss all this as mere antiquarianism. No body of men were more free from liturgical pedantry than the Provincial Synod which produced the new Scottish Prayer Book. But they knew the value of the old Prayer Book for its witness to the continuity of the Church's faith and worship, and they welcomed the chance of increasing the value of the new Book in that respect.

On the subject of "ritual" and ceremonial the Scottish Prayer Book is discreetly reticent. But even in this department something has been done, by recasting the rubrical directions of the Prayer Book, to guide clergy and people in the conduct of worship. The time has not yet come for the establishment even of a permissive standard of ceremonial, but already a large measure of uniformity has been secured in Scotland; and even in England, the divergencies in ceremonial and ritual are becoming much less marked than they were thirty years ago. The rigid uniformity of Rome is a novelty that has no right to call itself Catholic. Rich variety rather than narrow uniformity is the distinguishing mark of the Scottish Prayer Book. Its superiority to the English Prayer Book of 1662 is best recognised by a visit to some church in England where it is still used without modification, with its undeviating "Dearly Beloved Brethren", its heavy State Prayers, its long and monotonous Litany, its Ten Commandments and meagre Consecration Prayer, its unsatisfactory Form of Baptism, and its cold Burial Service. Yet this was all that Keble and Pusey ever had. Was it because they used what they had with more faithfulness that they gained a saintliness and an unselfishness which so greatly exceeds our own?

CHAPTER IX

# Sacred Learning and Sacred Art

At the beginning of the nineteenth century two essential elements in the Christian religion had almost entirely disappeared from popular religion in England, the institutional and the historic. The Church, the Sacraments and the ministry were disparaged as mere outward forms with which a Christian might dispense without loss; institutional Christianity was not the real thing. Similarly, the historic facts of Christianity were pushed aside in the interest of a narrow conception of faith, and the Gospel instead of containing truth to be taught became an appeal to be caught. "Only believe" was the jargon of the time; pietism was the whole of religion, theology its enemy. Faith was the sole requisite in religion, the intellectual and the aesthetic had no place there. Hence both sacred learning and sacred art, which throughout the ages had been the handmaids of faith, sank dishonoured in the dust.

The Oxford Movement is rightly described as a Catholic revival, because it rescued Christian religion from this narrow pietism by shewing that Christian institutions are an essential part of the

Gospel, that doctrine is the Church's interpretation of historic fact and that outward forms are inseparable from spiritual realities.

Keble, Newman and Pusey brought a new experience to their University when they taught young men that in the Gospel there was something to think about and talk about; a great Divine institution with its age-long history, its sacraments, its liturgy, its martyrs, its confessors; a massive body of truth contained in Scripture and expressed in Creeds, in Councils, in Articles of Faith; a method of Christian living by which confession, meditation, prayer, thanksgiving could be rationally commended for the imitation of Christ. From the first the Oxford Movement was, as we have seen, intellectual as well as spiritual. It spread through the printing press as well as through the pulpit. The Church was seen as a home for scholars as well as for saints. To the student vast fields of enquiry in Scripture interpretation, in theology, in history, in liturgy were opened out. To the average man and woman the Christian religion suddenly became interesting; there was something for ordinary people to think and speak about, where before there had only been silencing phrases of evangelical piety.

The intellectual energy of the early Tractarians was prodigious. Hardly a year passed without a book, sometimes two or three, appearing under the name of Keble, Pusey, Neale, or Isaac Williams. Less known men also played their part. Charles Marriott was one of these, a martyr to the cause of Christian truth, writing little himself but a born scholar who devoted himself to research, proof correction and the drudgery of the press on behalf of others. It was he who saw most of the vast Library of Anglo-Catholic Theology through the press, and yet found time to write more than a score of letters to George Forbes in Scotland about the service of Compline for Bishop Torry's Prayer Book. Bishop Forbes was a true Puseyite in this respect; a tremendous worker, who, with a large congregation in his charge as well as a diocese, devoted nearly a third of his day to study and wrote liturgical and theological works which would have filled up the full time of an average man for twenty years. Provost Cazenove in Cumbrae was another scholar who stood in the true succession of Tractarian learning, a marvel of erudition whose work for the most part lies buried in the *Dictionary of Christian Biography* and in reviews and magazines. William Bright of Glenalmond, a poet whose hymn "And now, O Father, mindful of the Love" supplies a finer interpretation of Eucharistic sacrifice than any treatise, was a third scholar, a gift of Oxford, like Forbes and Cazenove, to the Scottish Church. But, alas, he was too dangerous for the Scottish bishops, who failed to see in the brilliant sub-warden of Trinity College, Glenalmond, the future Professor of Ecclesiastical History with a dozen volumes to his credit, and asked him to resign his post. The treatment of these three brilliant men is a sad reflection upon the appreciation of the Scottish Church for sacred learning. Forbes was tried for false doctrine and all but condemned, Bright was invited to leave Glenalmond, and Cazenove was left in the obscurity of Cumbrae, unrecognised and unknown, for over twenty years.

But the revival of sacred learning was not without its effect in the Episcopal Church of Scotland, and from 1860 onwards there were numbers of the clergy, active-minded and well informed, whose intellectual energy was inspired by the work of the Tractarians and their successors.

The ritual troubles in England for a time produced a fighting spirit which was not favourable to the pursuit of learning; but in 1875, when a group of young scholars, Gore, Aubrey Moore, Illingworth, Talbot, and Scott Holland, was resident in Oxford, intellectual interest revived and once more became the distinction of the Movement resulting in the volume of essays entitled *Lux Mundi* (1889), which went through fourteen editions. And to-day almost all the most constructive scholars in the Church of England are those who find in the Catholic revival their inspiration to elucidate and commend Christian truth.

The Puritan fear of the external and the material, as hostile or distracting to the inward and the spiritual, gripped the minds of the English-speaking people for many years. It could justify itself by the plausible plea that beautiful buildings, stately ceremonial, rich vestments and jewelled chalices did not save the Church of the Middle Ages from grave corruptions of the Gospel and from low standards of life. Simple minds went further and saw in the Reformation the recovery of the spiritual by the destruction of the material; the beautiful was the enemy of the true and the good. There can be little doubt that in Scotland at the Reformation beautiful churches were defaced and works of art were destroyed by men who conscientiously believed that these things were, if not positively evil in themselves, dangerous to religion. In England the Reformation proceeded on Catholic lines, and the rubric in the Prayer Book directing that chancels "shall remain as in times past" maintained a continuity in architecture and in art which was almost entirely lost in Scotland. Nevertheless even in England the condition of church buildings and the externals of worship at the beginning of the nineteenth century were deplorable. Four-sided structures were intruded into the chancel for the accommodation and seclusion of the squires and their families; hideous galleries destroyed the design and proportion, as plaster and whitewash defaced the walls, of parish churches; the three-decker pulpit was thrust in front of the chancel, and the Altar in many churches was no more than a table covered with a velvet cloth and devoid of any symbol of the Christian faith.

It is impossible to exaggerate the change brought about by the refining influence of Tractarian teaching. It began quietly with a more seemly and reverent rendering of the services. Soon the spirit of the Movement changed the slovenly and uninspiring methods of conducting public worship, and then gradually the arts one by one came back to serve the cause of Christ. In Scotland church architecture was quite dead in the early part of the nineteenth century, and the churches in Cumbrae, Perth and Dundee, which were the first fruits of the Oxford Movement, were the work of English architects who, whatever their deficiencies, expressed in their designs the worshipful spirit as few architects in Scotland can do to-day, even with seventy years of experience of the revival behind them.

The period from 1860 to 1880 gave Scottish architects their opportunity of shewing what they could do, for in those years a large number of our churches were erected. But it cannot be said that they rose much above the conventional, probably because they had not schooled themselves, as English architects did, to appreciate the purposes for which church buildings are erected. Nevertheless our churches to-day are far more appropriate to their sacred uses than the barn-like structures which they displaced. The National War Memorial may be claimed as a product of the Movement, for Sir Robert Lorimer, its architect, was trained by Bodley, an architect in whose eyes a church was nothing if it failed to look a house of God and a house of prayer.

Church music developed more rapidly than architecture in sense, in taste, and in technique. The leading Tractarians being themselves poets and hymn-writers, it was natural that there should arise musicians able and eager to set to music the hymns of Keble, Neale, Bright and others. Of these Dr Dykes, a strong Tractarian and one of the finest organists and composers of his time, was the victim of bitter persecution in Durham for no better reason than that he stood for the Catholic principles of the Church of England. The devotional spirit and fine taste of Dykes were carried to Edinburgh by T. H. Collinson, organist of St Mary's Cathedral, Edinburgh, who did more than any man in Scotland to inspire the music of the Church with the true spirit of praise and holy fear; to this saintly musician the "effects" and tricks of the professional were abhorrent; his organ stool became a kind of Altar at which he was like one engaged in holy mysteries.

How strange it now seems to recall the time when Bishop Forbes, greatly daring, introduced what was called "the choral service" which meant singing the versicles and responses, the Psalms and Canticles and occasionally an anthem. In the *Directory of the Episcopal Church in Scotland* for the year 1878 it is taken for a sign of Catholicity to describe church services as "choral", or "partly choral", or as "plain except on Festivals when fully choral". In England the tradition of Church music had only to be revived; in Scotland it had to be created or rather, imported from England. Congregations suffered much from the musical efforts of these primitive choirs and organists. But when Church music became good enough to disprove the prevailing view that it was a hindrance rather than a help to worship, the interest of congregations was aroused. It took some years before musicians turned their attention to the development of this new interest and once again the inspiration came from England.

The School of English Church Music, in no sense a party society, may be described as Catholic in its aims, for no society has done so much to make plainsong tunes interesting to choirs, and plainsong hymns loved by congregations. Above all, it has taught people to see the obvious which they seldom do until it is forced upon their notice. The obvious in this case is that a liturgical service is a unity made up of various elements, praise, prayer, meditation, thanksgiving, and that the work of the musician is to manifest the artistic unity of the whole by seeing that the music fits and expresses every part of the service. No one can teach a choir to chant the Psalms intelligently unless he understands their meaning, nor can anyone train a body of singers for a choral Eucharist unless he understands, at least to some extent, the structure of the service. This was the very principle which the early Tractarians believed to be fundamental. Here, they said, in the Prayer Book are the services of the Catholic Church; they are not perfect but they are sufficient, provided they are properly rendered. Had the ceremonial or "ritual" movement accepted Pusey's guidance and advanced, as he wished, more thoughtfully and slowly, there might have been established a standard of worship, dignified, intelligible, and reverent, which might have been universally followed, instead of a number of "uses" full of seams and patches proclaiming their foreign origin. If Church music in the future continues to quicken the liturgical sense, it may lead to a finer appreciation of what ceremonial ought to be as the expression, not of modern Roman Catholic services, but of the more Catholic worship of the Anglican Church.

Along with the advance in architectural and musical taste there has gone also a desire to see the

Church worthily provided with furnishings for the conduct of worship. The old red velvet has disappeared from our Altars and its place taken by Altar coverings designed by competent artists. Here the Sisterhoods, which, as we have seen, were the direct result of the Oxford Movement, have led the way by shewing how the needlewoman may consecrate her skill to the worship of the Most High.

Sacred art has made great advances during the last fifty years. In the days of Bishop Forbes it was but in its infancy, but its true spirit was there, the spirit of consecration. If those who followed him had been possessed of this redeeming spirit, they would have hesitated before defacing their churches with bad glass, eagle lecterns, crude vestments, pitchpine pews and the like. It was the revival of Catholic principles that brought artists back to their function of adorning the worship of God "with all manner of cunning workmanship". "All art", says Ruskin, "is praise", and Christian art should be the great Christian Gloria to God "in the Church and through Christ Jesus".

CHAPTER X

# The Worth of Catholic Principles To-day

The *Tracts for the Times* are not tracts for our times. Pusey's theological writings are for the most part dead stock, reposing side by side with Keble's and most of Newman's, in the studies of the older clergy or on the shelves of University libraries; even Newman's sermons are read less for their substance than for their style. We can appreciate the Oxford Movement and its principles by reading the letters of the leaders rather than their formal writings. Keble, Newman and Pusey were admirable letter writers, always intimate, frank, revealing and extraordinarily human. To the modern reader their published books appear dry; the treatment is academic, the appeal to Scripture old-fashioned, the fear of rationalism excessive. Does it follow therefore that the principles which they taught with such courage and at such cost to themselves are as antiquated as the expression of them in Tractarian books? By no means.

The faith once delivered to the saints remains the same, though it can no longer be commended by Pusey's arguments or in Newman's polished sentences. The direct successors of Keble and Pusey, Gore and his friends who wrote *Lux Mundi* in 1889, are as different in thought and expression from their predecessors as Mr Trevelyan, the historian, is from his great-uncle, Lord Macaulay. Mr Studdert Kennedy's books would have made Pusey shudder, yet not only is his teaching the same in substance as Keble's, but his method of presenting it through the mind to the soul is also similar, though his style and language are as unlike the Tractarians' as Masefield's poetry is to Tennyson's. Let us now briefly consider some of the truths prominent in the teaching of the Tractarians. We may begin with the great fundamentals of the faith, though these were assumed by Pusey and Keble rather than enunciated with any fullness. The popular conceptions of God, of the Incarnation, of the Atonement, underwent a great change as the movement gained strength. The last vestiges of Calvinism were stripped away from theology, and the Fatherhood of God, the Incarnation of Christ as the revelation of Divine Love, the Sacrifice of Calvary for all mankind, were expressed with a tenderness, an intimacy and a reality undreamed of in days when religion was either frozen in conventionality or heated in the artificial, unhealthy atmosphere of unintelligent evangelicalism. Probably the indirect teaching of the Oxford leaders on these great themes, combined with the intense reality of their own personal religion, produced a greater effect on the thought of the time than the direct handling of those particular truths with which their names are associated.

Most prominent among these was their conception of the Church as a Divine institution established to express the mind and will of Christ in the world. Ecclesiasticism was abhorrent to Keble and Pusey; the Church of England in their day reeked of it in its worst form of outward display and inward snobbery. St Paul's title of the Church as the Body of Christ was no mere metaphor to the Oxford leaders. To see the Church of England as the hands and feet, the lips and tongue of the living Christ was the one ambition that filled their hearts. The Protestant idea that men could follow Christ as Lord apart from the Church was in their view a misrepresentation of history, a flat contradiction of Apostolic tradition and a defiance of the social nature of mankind. Spiritual ideas *in vacuo* can have no permanence; they must find expression in institutions, and if men reject the Catholic Church they are sure sooner or later to establish counterfeits of their own in its place. The question, "Did Christ found a Church?" is not answered by pointing to the absence of the word in the earliest written Gospel. Had there been no Christian community, there would have been no Gospel according to St Mark. The New Testament books were written within and not without the Beloved Community, preserved by it and gradually recognised as Canonical by it. A Churchless Christianity is a novelty which cannot be read into or behind the Acts of the Apostles and the Apostolic Epistles, and is condemned by the aims and methods of Christ as revealed in the Gospel. Christ Himself was brought up in a Divine community and the superficial idea that He was a revolutionary out to destroy is false to the record of the Evangelists. The Divine Ecclesia of the New Testament is a continuation of the old, just as Jesus Himself is a fulfilment of the promise of God to the Fathers. Hence St Paul and St Peter carry over and apply to Christians those social titles which were descriptive of the Jewish Church—"the Saints", "the elect", "the New Israel" "the Israel of God", "a royal priesthood". The Church idea cannot be detached from the writings of the New Testament. Why then do people imagine this vain thing, a Churchless religion? Chiefly because the Church, as they see it in the world, appears so unlike both its Master and the Church of the Apostles. That was the real difficulty of Newman with the Church of England. In his life it seemed a respectable, worldly, unadventurous body with not even the desire to be like the Church of the

New Testament. Did he discover a closer resemblance in the Church of Rome? Far from it. He simply learned to accept its limitations, pleading on its behalf the weakness of human nature. Every new sect that arises justifies itself on the ground that it is nearer the New Testament pattern than any other. There is and always must be a certain clash between the Church as it exists in the world and the Church as it is meant to be, the Body of Christ. The mission of the Church and the duty of every member is so to "walk worthy of the vocation wherewith we are called" that the Church may act and be the Body of Christ.

An exact reproduction of the Apostolic Church to-day is impossible for two reasons: first, because we cannot tell in any detailed way what the Church of the New Testament was like; we can only discern its beliefs, its Sacramental rites, its ministry and discipline, its moral principles; secondly, because apart from these, change and development are assumed in the New Testament as inevitable.

The concern of the Tractarians with the ministry was primarily religious, not ecclesiastical, and was bound up with the idea of the Church as a living organism. The Apostolic Succession was the guarantee that the ministry was not simply a convenience of the Church which might be changed at any time. Here the conflict of opinion among scholars to-day is sharper than on any other Catholic doctrine. Some would hold that the living organism of the Church first grew for itself the hand of the Diaconate, that a second hand came out in the Presbyterate, and finally that there evolved from the Presbyters the directing hand of the Episcopate, the whole process being initiated and guided by the Apostles, and completed by the end of the first century. Roman Catholics under Newman's theory of development would carry this process a stage further and see in the Papacy a natural growth from the bishops. The Tractarians, however, were not inclined to this theory, though Newman, even in his Anglican days, was feeling his way towards it. They would have argued that if God meant to give his Church an infallible head, He would not have waited till 1870 to declare it infallible nor till the sixteenth century to empower it to call a General Council, nor till the eighth century to claim authority over the whole Church. Nevertheless, the evolutionary theory of the ministry is quite orthodox, though its application to the late arrival of the Papacy tends to identify it with "modernism".

The historical problem narrows itself down to this question, How can we reconcile the three orders of bishops, priests and deacons which unquestionably existed in Asia in the time of St Ignatius (A.D. 117) with the ministry which we find in the Epistles and the Acts of the Apostles, say, between A.D. 50 and 80? If the threefold ministry was a mere accident or a sacerdotal novelty, then the whole Church of Christ was for centuries precariously poised upon an accident or a mistake. Such an inference is quite incongruous with the fearless confidence with which she faced and overcame the powers of darkness in the first three centuries. It is more reasonable to see in the Apostles the predecessors of that ministry of bishops to which no alternative appeared till the sixteenth century and then only in Scotland and some parts of the Continent.

It is possible and even easy to deride this Catholic conception of the ministry. But on one fundamental point the vast majority of Christian people are agreed. A Christian minister cannot impose himself and his ministrations upon the Church of God. An inward call to minister in the Church is not sufficient. So far there is no dispute; the ministry is "given" in the sense that no man can put himself into it. He must be given his authority by those already in possession of it. Spiritual powers of ministry are bestowed in Apostolic fashion by the Spirit of God acting in the rite of Ordination through the laying-on of hands. Here Presbyterians are at one with Episcopalians; both believe in Apostolic Succession, the one through presbyters, the other through bishops. If that be so, it should not pass the wit of man to effect some real combination of the two. The real principle of Apostolic succession lies, not primarily in questions about the "validity" of Sacraments or the "transmission of grace", but in the fact that Holy Orders are given, not taken. Are they best given with bishops or without them? The practice of the whole Church of Christ for at least fourteen hundred years and of the greater part for eighteen hundred years is for Episcopacy.

The Tractarians, however, were more interested in the religious than the theological question of the ministry. The genuineness of Holy Orders placed upon the recipients responsibilities which could be discharged only by men who were ready to fling personal ambition, comfort and ease to the winds: and whatever else Apostolic Succession accomplished, it transformed the conception of the ministry in the Church of England from a worldly career of comparative ease, with "livings", "dignities" and other rewards of "a profession", into a laborious life of study, of prayer, of feeding the flock of Christ. The Oxford Movement brought about a revolution in the lives of clergy. No priest could be lazy, no bishop easy-going or slack who professed to follow the path marked out and trodden by Keble and Pusey.

The "givenness" of the Sacraments was the third truth which gained a new significance from the Oxford Movement. In particular the Eucharist was the meat and drink of the Tractarians and their successors. The theology of that Sacrament was of interest only as preserving the spiritual and religious reality. The "Real Presence" in the Eucharist was to Keble, Pusey and Forbes not simply a dogma; it was a gift ready to be bestowed at every Altar, the gift of Christ's Body and Blood. The Sacrifice of the Eucharist was no less real an offering to God, through which by Christ's appointment the one Sacrifice of the Cross was appropriated by the many. It might have been well if the word "real" had been attached to sacrifice and omitted from "Presence", for no Presence of Christ could be unreal, whereas there had been sacrifices of bulls and goats which might be described as unreal compared with the real spiritual sacrifice which commemorates the Sacrifice of the Cross.

Much has been written upon the mystery of the Eucharist since Keble published his treatise on *Eucharistic Adoration* and Pusey his work on the *Real Presence*. They found the language of the Greek and Latin fathers sufficient to draw out the implications of the New Testament on the subject, and believed that by adhering to patristic forms of thought they came closer to the Apostolic doctrine than by a new interpretation with a new vocabulary. We are not content with the ideas and the language of the past. Just as we have abandoned old theories of Justification which were based on a metaphor rather than a fact, so we have left behind us those literal ideas about Christ's natural Body which left their mark in the "Black Rubric" of the Prayer Book. We are no longer shocked at the Roman doctrine of transubstantiation because we know that Aristotle's idea of substance which produced it is, at the best tenable, and at the worst harmless.

We have our own ways of expressing and commending the reality both of the offering and of the Presence in the Eucharist, and our liturgical forms are large enough to hold these and much besides which future enquiry may discover.

In 1851 Pusey was inhibited by Bishop Wilberforce from officiating in his diocese because he had told a penitent after confession to say some parts of the 119th Psalm as an act of amendment. Keble, now sixty years of age, hearing of this wrote to Pusey, "I wish I were a fairy to send the Bishop a rosary on which he should be forced to say the 119th Psalm (which he calls a choral hymn) every day of his life. Look at the 23rd and 161st verses of it, my dearest Pusey". Pusey, more serious than his playful friend, begged his bishop to prosecute him at law and so prove him wrong, at the same time pledging himself to defray all the legal expenses!

Controversy on this subject is happily ended. Experience, reinforced by psychology, has shewn the value of private confession and absolution. Where it has been in abeyance, dangerous substitutes have been found for it in the enquiry room of the evangelical preacher and in the public confessions of individuals in the presence of a group. No doubt private confession, like many other laudable practices, may be degraded. Its so-called psychological value may reduce it to mere self-discipline. The root of the matter lies where the Tractarians always said it lay, in the reality of man's repentance on the one hand and of Divine forgiveness on the other.

CHAPTER XI

# The Catholic Movement in the Presbyterian Churches

When in 1833 Keble's assize sermon was the talk of Oxford, a young minister of the Established Church of Scotland was conducting public worship in a small chapel-of-ease at Arbroath. Ten years later his great abilities carried him to the important charge of Old Greyfriars, Edinburgh, whose minister had just "gone out" at the Disruption. In 1846 he was appointed Professor of Biblical Criticism in Edinburgh University, a position which he held along with his ministerial charge. A fire destroyed the old church of Greyfriars in 1845, and Dr Lee (as he had now become) determined to erect a new one which would bear more resemblance to the churches of older times. Delays, however, were interposed and the church, one of the first Presbyterian churches in Scotland to be designed in the Gothic style, was not erected till 1857.

Dr Lee had long chafed at the beggarly type of service which, according to Dr Story, Lee's biographer, passed for worship in those days; a bleak and dreary formality in which the opening and closing prayers, ostensibly extempore, rambled on in the same meaningless phrases from year to year, the Lord's Prayer never being used by the minister, and in some churches the Bible never read. As late as 1856 the General Assembly had to issue an order enjoining the reading of a portion of the Old and New Testament at every diet of worship. In 1857 Dr Lee began his reform of Presbyterian worship by introducing into his new church a service book and inviting his people to kneel at prayer and stand at praise. These innovations raised a great outcry and Dr Lee was called to account both by his Presbytery and the General Assembly for "playing at Episcopacy". His gravest offence was the reading of prayers from a book. Dr Lee deferred to the General Assembly and for some years gave up his service book, but in 1863 he returned to it, at the same time infuriating his opponents still more by introducing a harmonium into his church. He was arraigned before the Assembly in 1864 and in a notable speech, which won him a majority, declared, "I would far rather that you forbade me to read my sermons than my prayers. It is far more natural to read a prayer than to read a sermon. You look men in the face when you speak to them but it is of no consequence where you are looking when you are speaking to the King Eternal, Immortal, Invisible".

How far Dr Lee's campaign for liturgical worship was directly affected by the Oxford Movement it is hard to say. But there is no question that he admired the Book of Common Prayer, and was familiar with the changes in public worship which had resulted from the re-discovery of the book both in England and in Scotland. It is, however, also true that he viewed with alarm the growing progress of the Scottish Episcopal Church and rightly judged that one reason for the attachment of an increasing number of "the gentry" to the Church was the spiritual reality and beauty of liturgical worship. It was partly to arrest the flow of educated people to Episcopacy which was strong at the time that, in 1864, Dr Lee published his work on the Reform of the Church, in which he advocated the observance of Christmas, Good Friday and Easter, "instead of the absurd practice of local fast days". In the following year he further outraged the Puritanical feeling of the time by introducing an organ into his church. He was again called to account, and the famous Greyfriars' case was still proceeding in the Assembly when he met with an accident which proved fatal in 1867.

The movement thus begun to secure the outward decencies of worship resulted in the formation of the Church Service Society in 1864, which, however, was wise enough not to commit itself to Dr Lee's somewhat crude service book. This society at first confined its work to the revival and enrichment of Knox's Book of Common Order, but in 1904 it departed from the traditions of Presbyterianism and published the Scottish Prayer Book of 1637, commonly known as "Laud's Liturgy" under the editorship of Dr Cooper. Towards the close of the 'eighties it appeared to a number of distinguished ministers that Dr Lee had begun his reform at the wrong end. Slovenly worship was an effect, not a cause. An aesthetic type of service, however close in form to ancient liturgies, might look and be no more than a new patch on a threadbare garment. There must be the Catholic mind, imbued with the deep mysteries of the faith, before worship could naturally clothe itself in outward forms of order, beauty and reverence.

In order, therefore, to divert interest to more important matters than the minor accessories of worship, the Scottish Church Society was formed in 1892 by Professor Milligan of Aberdeen, Dr John McLeod of Govan and others, with the object of bringing out the Catholic elements of faith, order and discipline in the standards of the Established Church. This was a return to the method of the Oxford Movement which, as has been shewn, aimed at reviving the Church's faith and life and not simply at improving the externals of worship. Dr Milligan's works on *The Resurrection of Christ* and *The Ascension and Heavenly Priesthood of*

*Christ* gave a strong lead in this direction, and revealed a new appreciation of Christian doctrine. In particular the Aberdeen professor treated the conception of Eucharistic sacrifice with all Keble's depth of feeling and with no less power. In 1895 Dr McLeod wrote a paper for the society in which he boldly advocated the weekly Eucharist and the daily service.

Dr Cooper in the field of history and Dr Wotherspoon in that of liturgy and theology added strength to this new movement. Both, like the Tractarians, were deeply religious as well as scholarly men, and, like them also, profoundly interested in the cause of Christian unity. Dr Wotherspoon, one of the saintliest of men and a theologian of real constructive ability, wrote his last book on the Sacraments with the hope that it might contribute something to a union between the Church of Scotland and the Anglican communion, by shewing how much common ground there was on this subject between the two Churches. In spite, however, of the labours of these and other men of yore, the Scottish Church Society has not exercised a wide influence on the thought of the Presbyterian Churches. The reason for this may be that there exists no authoritative Presbyterian manual of faith and practice similar to the Book of Common Prayer, in which the average member can find a clear statement of the beliefs of his

Church. It is not easy for him to see that the Presbyterian Church is other than a new creation of the Reformation, when Episcopacy, Confirmation, the use of the Creeds, frequent Communion, the observance of the Christian Year, and a liturgy for clergy and people all disappeared. Many of these beliefs and practices have now been revived but they appear to the majority of Presbyterians to be importations from the Church of England, just as the service of Benediction, a post-Reformation novelty even in Rome, seems to the average Anglican to be an importation from the Church of Rome.

One of the longest steps towards a union of Presbyterianism with Episcopacy will be taken when, on the one hand, the General Assembly of the Church of Scotland provides its people with an authoritative manual of faith and devotion that will lift the masses of the Scottish people out of the nebulous Christianity with which for the present so many are content, and when, on the other hand, the Church of England sets itself to create unity where it should begin, in its own house. The influence of the Oxford Movement on Scottish Presbyterianism has been indirect rather than direct, aesthetic more than doctrinal, nevertheless it has brought the Church of Scotland nearer the Church of England by familiarising its members with Catholic truths and practices which, even thirty years ago, would have been scorned as rags of Popery.

It would be quite possible for a dozen clergy drawn from each side to find a basis for union even upon the question of the ministry, if they considered the opinions of none save themselves; but they could not at present devise any synthesis of Episcopacy and Presbyterianism which a majority of the rank and file of the clergy on both sides would not resolutely oppose. In the seventeenth century Scotland had some experience of a cheap unity brought about by suppressing rather than expressing truth. No abiding remedy for healing the fissures in the Body of Christ lies in that direction. Comprehension, not compromise, inclusion, not exclusion, must be the method. It was in this spirit that Pusey and Bishop Forbes faced the impossible task of union with the Roman Catholic Church and Keble contemplated union with the Non-conformist Churches in England. All three were disappointed, for prejudice was strong in their day. Our danger lies in lack of conviction rather than in preconceived ideas, in the *amour propre* of ministers rather than in the blind conservatism of the people. Yet who can doubt that one Church, one Faith, one Lord, one Baptism, is the will of Christ?

For EU product safety concerns, contact us at Calle de José Abascal, 56–1°, 28003 Madrid, Spain or eugpsr@cambridge.org.

www.ingramcontent.com/pod-product-compliance
Ingram Content Group UK Ltd.
Pitfield, Milton Keynes, MK11 3LW, UK
UKHW020313140625
459647UK00018B/1860

* 9 7 8 1 1 0 7 4 3 7 8 8 3 *